PROPERTY
& TAXATION

PROPERTY
& TAXATION

A Practical Guide
to Saving Tax
on Your Property
Investments

Jimmy B. Prince

Wrightbooks

First published 2011 by Wrightbooks
an imprint of John Wiley & Sons Australia, Ltd
42 McDougall Street, Milton Qld 4064

Office also in Melbourne

Typeset in Adobe Garamond 12.5/15.5pt

© Jimmy B. Prince 2011

The moral rights of the author have been asserted

National Library of Australia Cataloguing-in-Publication entry

Author:	Prince, Jimmy B.
Title:	Property and taxation: a practical guide to saving tax on your property investments / Jimmy B. Prince.
ISBN:	9780730375524 (pbk.)
Notes:	Includes index.
Subjects:	Real estate investment — Taxation — Australia. Real property and taxation — Australia.
Dewey Number:	336.220994

Cover image ($100 note) © iStockphoto.com/robynmac

All extracts taken from Australian Acts of Law © Commonwealth of Australia 2010. All legislation herein is reproduced by permission but does not purport to be the official or authorised version. It is subject to Commonwealth of Australia copyright. The *Copyright Act 1968* permits certain reproduction and publication of Commonwealth legislation and judgements. In particular, section 182A of the Act enables a complete copy to be made by or on behalf of a particular person. For reproduction or publication beyond that permitted by the Act, permission should be sought in writing. Requests should be addressed to Commonwealth Copyright Administration, Attorney-General's Department, Robert Garran Offices, National Circuit, Bardon, ACT 2600, or posted at http://www.ag.gov.au/cca.

Printed in China by Printplus Limited.

10 9 8 7 6 5 4 3 2

Disclaimer
The material in this publication is of the nature of general comment only, and does not represent professional advice. It is not intended to provide specific guidance for particular circumstances and it should not be relied on as the basis for any decision to take action or not take action on any matter which it covers. Readers should obtain professional advice where appropriate, before making any such decision. To the maximum extent permitted by law, the author and publisher disclaim all responsibility and liability to any person, arising directly or indirectly from any person taking or not taking action based upon the information in this publication.

Contents

About the author

Jim Prince is a fellow of CPA Australia and a tax specialist. He is a former lecturer and tutor in income tax law at La Trobe University and teaches a number of wealth-creation courses for the Centre for Adult Education in Melbourne. He has authored several investment books including *Tax for Australians for Dummies* and *Shares & Taxation*, and has written articles for *Your Mortgage* magazine and <http://thebull.com.au>. In 2000 Jim was nominated for an Adult Learners Week 2000 outstanding tutor award.

In his earlier years Jim worked for the Australian Taxation Office and also consulted to CPA Australia 'Technicall'.

Preface

I always emphasise to participants in my wealth-creation courses that real estate is a key investment option that just about ticks all the boxes of an ideal investment. This is because property gives you the opportunity to receive a regular and reliable income flow plus capital growth. It can also be used as collateral to secure a loan to buy a quality share portfolio or another investment property.

There are also many taxation benefits that may interest you. Under Australian tax law your main residence is exempt from the capital gains tax (CGT) provisions, which means no tax is payable on any capital gain you make on the sale. This is great to know if you happen to be living in a location where property values are continually going up. But wait, there's more! The good news gets even better if you also own an investment property in a self-managed superannuation fund. This is because once you turn 60 and retire, the entire capital gain you make on the sale to fund your retirement is exempt from tax. On the other hand if you own a rental property, block of land or holiday home for more than 12 months, and you make a capital gain on the sale, only half the capital gain is taxable. The other half is exempt and excluded from your assessable income.

If you're a property investor and you own a rental property, expenses such as interest payments on a mortgage, borrowing costs, council rates and land taxes, insurance, repairs and depreciation are tax deductible. And you could qualify for a capital works deduction if your rental property was constructed after a certain date. Unfortunately, you can't claim these expenses if you own your main residence or a holiday home that you use for your personal use and enjoyment. But all is not lost! If you own a holiday home many of these expenses can be added to the property's cost base and can be used to reduce any capital gain you make on the sale.

Coming to terms with the different taxation issues associated with owning a rental property can at times be mind-boggling and difficult to understand. There are statutory laws and umpteen tax rulings governing what you can and can't claim as a tax deduction, and special rules to calculate a capital gain or capital loss. To complicate matters further, if you decide to buy a property with the intention to renovate and sell at a profit, the Tax Office may deem you to be carrying on a business of renovating properties. If this is the case the entire profit you make on the sale is liable to tax. So if you're contemplating doing a little property speculation you should seek professional advice on how you're likely to be taxed. Unfortunately, when it comes to tax you simply can't guess whether you're engaged in a profit-making activity or you're merely a property investor. If you get it wrong the Tax Office could impose stiff penalties.

This book explains in simple terms core tax principles with numerous tax tips, potential tax traps and practical case studies to reinforce the learning process. You'll also find some handy tax-planning tips that may appeal to you, plus a comprehensive list of legal citations to all the major tax cases relating to property transactions. Much emphasis is placed on the following core tax principles:

- how property speculators and property investors are taxed

- how your property transactions are taxed

- how to calculate a capital gain and capital loss

- the tax issues associated with owning a main residence

- investing in an overseas property

- borrowing to buy a property

- owning property in different legal structures

- record keeping and tax audits.

Throughout the book you'll have at your fingertips instant 'at a glance' information on core tax principles, plus references to taxation publications, tax rulings and tax determinations that tax professionals use to solve specific problems. You can quickly find these Tax Office publications and rulings on the Australian Taxation Office website. This practical guide to saving tax on property can be continually used to help you find a particular publication or ruling you may wish to consult from time to time.

The purpose of writing this book is to give you the basic skills (and confidence) to deal with the many taxation issues relating to real estate and to empower you to make property investment a working financial strategy for you.

Chapter 1

The Australian tax system and property: removing the mystique

When you invest in real estate you are effectively purchasing a future income stream (rent) and locking into potential capital growth opportunities if your property appreciates in value. As a general rule properties in good locations tend to double in value every seven to ten years. There are also significant taxation benefits linked with this category of investment that may interest you. In this chapter I cover the basics and guide you through the key tax principles relating to property transactions.

Landlords and tenants: rights and obligations

When you lease a rental property you are giving a tenant a legal right to occupy your property during the term of the lease. In return your tenant will pay you rent, usually on a monthly basis. The state and territory governments of Australia are the governing authorities responsible for regulating the real estate industry, and more particularly rental properties. So before you lease your property it's best to familiarise yourself with your local state or territory government Residential Tenancies Act. Incidentally, you can access guidelines setting out your legal rights and obligations on the internet—search for the keywords 'residential tenancies act'. The main rules and regulations that landlords and tenants must comply with are listed here.

At a glance: landlord obligations

Landlords must:

- prepare and give their tenants a written residential lease agreement setting out the terms of the lease

- ensure the rental property is clean and fit for human habitation

- install smoke alarms

- give their tenants vacant possession and privacy during the term of the lease

- obtain written permission from their tenants before entering the property during the term of the lease

- undertake any necessary repairs and maintenance to the property and, more particularly, fix any urgent defects (for instance a leaking roof)

- properly account for bond money received from tenants in accordance with the Residential Tenancies Act

- ensure the rental property is safe and secure (for instance by installing door and window locks)

- pay all council rates and land taxes when they become due and payable

- give a tenant 60 days' notice of an increase in rental payments.

At a glance: tenant obligations

Tenants must:

- pay the agreed amount of rent when it's due and payable

- keep the property clean and tidy

- not damage the property

- vacate the property when the lease expires.

Tenants are entitled to receive their bond money back on the termination of the lease (provided they do not damage the property or default on the rent).

In addition to the Residential Tenancies Act, landlords must also comply with the *Income Tax Assessment Act 1997*. They must disclose in their individual tax returns the taxable income they derive from leasing their rental property.

How the Australian tax system works

Under Australian law, tax is levied on your taxable income. The Income Tax Assessment Act defines 'taxable income' as 'total assessable income less allowable deductions'. For Individuals, tax is levied on your taxable income on a progressive basis. This means the more taxable income you derive, the more tax you're liable to pay. Property investors can claim a capital-works deduction for properties constructed after September 1987 (see Capital-works deductions on p. 12).

The amount of tax you actually pay depends on your marginal rates of tax (which can vary between 0 per cent and 45 per cent). Any tax payable is reduced by certain domestic tax offsets you may be entitled to claim (for instance a 'low income tax offset'). You may also be liable to a pay a Medicare levy if your taxable income is above a statutory amount. The Medicare levy is currently 1.5 per cent of your taxable income.

At a glance: how you're taxed

This is how the Australian tax system works:

- Resident individuals pay tax on a progressive basis at their marginal rates of tax, but the first $6000 you earn is tax-free.

- Non-residents pay tax at non-resident tax rates on income sourced in Australia (for instance, from a rental property located in Australia). Note: non-residents may need to seek government approval to buy real estate in Australia. For more details see the Foreign Investment Review Board website <www.firb.gov.au>.

- Capital gains are liable to tax at your marginal rates of tax, but you can claim a 50 per cent capital gains tax (CGT) discount if you hold CGT assets (for instance property) for more than 12 months (see chapter 4). One significant benefit is that your main residence is ordinarily exempt from the CGT provisions (see chapter 5).

- If you operate a small business and you sell your business premises or transfer it to your self-managed super fund, under the CGT concessions for small business, any capital gain you make on disposal may be concessionally taxed or exempt from tax (see chapters 4 and 8).

- Individuals can claim certain tax offsets (for instance, a spouse tax offset and a low income tax offset if their taxable income is below $67 500).

- Companies pay a flat 30 per cent rate of tax on the entire amount of taxable income they derive. This rate is expected to fall to 29 per cent in the 2013–14 financial year. But companies miss out on the 50 per cent CGT discount (see chapter 8).

- A partnership is not liable to pay tax. But all partnership income and losses must be distributed to the individual partners. Under Australian tax law, if you co-own a rental property you will be considered to be in partnership and, more particularly, in receipt of income jointly (see chapter 8).

- A trust must lodge a trust tax return but is not liable to pay tax. All trust net income is assessed as part of the income of either the trustee or beneficiaries. But a trust cannot distribute losses (see chapter 8).

- Complying superannuation funds pay a flat 15 per cent rate of tax. But all withdrawals from a super fund after you reach 60 years of age and retire are tax free, which is good to know if your self managed super fund owns an investment property (see chapter 8).

 Tax tip

If you want to find out your current marginal rates of tax you can visit the Australian Taxation Office website <www.ato.gov.au>. Go to 'Find a rate or calculator' then 'Individual income tax rates'.

Coming to terms with self-assessment

Australia's tax system operates on a self-assessment basis. Under self-assessment when you lodge your annual tax return for individuals, the Australian Taxation Office

(ATO) will ordinarily accept its contents as being true and correct. Apart from correcting any obvious errors (for instance adding mistakes) no further action is taken. However, the Tax Office reserves the right to audit your tax affairs. So to ensure you're complying with the Income Tax Assessment Act, the Tax Office will regularly check income tax returns against external real estate property data (see chapter 9).

The Tax Office has provided a comprehensive list of tax-related errors or omissions relating to real estate (see chapter 9). The most common ones are listed here.

CGT-related issues

Common errors include:

- not declaring capital gains on the disposal of holiday homes and rental properties (see chapter 4)

- claiming a main-residence exemption while residing in another state and claiming a main residence there as well (see chapter 5)

- using the wrong dates when working out the capital gains or losses from selling a property (see chapter 4).

Income tax–related issues

Common errors include:

- not declaring all your rental income (see chapter 3)

- not keeping full and accurate records such as receipts for renovations, interest and insurance costs, building plans, market valuations and contracts (see chapter 9)

- overstating interest deductions by including amounts relating to borrowing expenses (see chapter 7)

- claiming deductions for a property that is not genuinely available for rent (see chapter 3)

- not claiming partial deductions where a property is rented for only part of the year (see chapter 3)

- claiming initial repair or renovation costs as repair and maintenance costs rather than correctly attributing these to the property's cost base (see chapter 3)

- incorrectly apportioning deductions related to private borrowings or travel (see chapter 3)

- incorrectly claiming deductions against rental income for legal and other costs that should be treated as capital expenditure (see chapter 3).

To avoid incurring any potential tax penalties for noncompliance, it's best that you keep proper records and receipts to verify and substantiate what you disclose in your tax return. It's also recommended that you seek professional advice from a recognised tax adviser if in doubt.

Tax tip

The Australian Taxation Office is the federal government authority responsible for administering the Income Tax Assessment Act. The Tax Office regularly issues Tax Office publications, Income Tax Rulings, Tax Determinations and ATO Interpretative Decisions to explain tax principles that need to be clarified and brought to your attention; you will find them referenced throughout this book. It also publishes fact sheets and booklets on specific topics such as real estate. These publications are free of charge, and are issued to help you to comply with Australia's complex tax laws. You can download these publications and rulings from the ATO website <www.ato.gov.au>.

Getting professional help

If you're experiencing difficulty complying with the numerous tax requirements relating to real estate, you can seek a private ruling from the Tax Office. If you do this, the Tax Office will examine your request and give you a written response outlining how they would interpret the law on the issue you have raised. There is no fee for this service. By the way, you'll have to follow the opinion they give you, unless you consider you have a strong legal argument to suggest otherwise. If you disagree with the ruling you'll need to lodge a formal objection (see chapter 9).

Alternatively, you can seek the services of a recognised tax adviser (registered tax agent or a legal practitioner). A recognised tax adviser is a person who is authorised to give you advice on managing your tax affairs. A tax adviser can prepare and lodge a tax return on your behalf, attend a Tax Office audit and lodge an objection if you're dissatisfied with your notice of assessment (see chapter 9). The fees charged for these services are ordinarily tax-deductible expenses.

 Tax trap

If you do not lodge your individual tax return by 31 October you could be liable to pay a late lodgment penalty. You can avoid this penalty if you visit a registered tax agent. This is because tax agents are given a general extension of time to lodge income tax returns on behalf of their clients.

 Tax tip

There are two ways you can lodge your tax return. You can fill out the paper tax form included in the *TaxPack* for individuals and post it to your local Tax Office, or you can lodge your tax return online using e-tax. You can get a copy of the *TaxPack* for individuals from your local newsagent or you can contact your local Tax Office.

Checklist: property and taxation

The following checklist provides a quick overview of the key taxation issues associated with investing in real estate. These issues will be discussed in greater detail in later chapters.

Rental income

Rent is normally payable on a monthly basis. Under Australian tax law rental income is ordinarily liable to tax when the rent is paid or credited to your account (see chapter 3).

Allowable deductions

Under Australian tax law, losses and outgoings incurred in the course of deriving your assessable income (for instance, rent), or necessarily incurred in carrying on a business (for instance, if you're a property developer or property speculator) for the purposes of deriving assessable income, are tax-deductible expenses. But you can't claim a loss or outgoing to the extent that it is capital, private or domestic in nature (see chapter 3). The most common expenses associated with income-producing properties are listed here:

- capital works deductions (building write-off deductions)
- council rates
- depreciation (decline in value)

- insurance

- interest on a mortgage to buy a rental property

- land taxes

- repairs and maintenance.

Interest on borrowings

Interest on borrowings to purchase an income-producing property is ordinarily a tax-deductible expense. A partial deduction is allowed if the property is only partly used to derive assessable income. For instance, you own a property consisting of 10 rooms of equal size and you use five rooms to derive your assessable income. As only part of the property is used to derive assessable income, you can only claim a partial deduction (in this case 50 per cent). Under Australian tax law if your interest payments (plus other expenses) exceed your rental income, the net loss can be deducted from other assessable income you derive (for instance from your salary and wages, business profits and investment income). This is commonly known as negative gearing (see chapter 7).

Capital-works deductions

Under Australian tax law, income-producing buildings constructed after 15 September 1987 qualify for a special tax deduction under the capital works provisions. Under these provisions you can claim a 2.5 per cent capital-works deduction over a 40-year period. The rate increases to 4 per cent if you purchase an industrial property.

This special tax deduction also applies to any structural improvements or alterations you make to a property (for instance, you add an extra room or make substantial renovations to your rental property; see chapter 3).

Capital gains

Under Australian tax law unrealised capital gains are not liable to tax. This means it's possible for you to own a property that's continually increasing in value, and no tax is payable until there's a CGT event. A CGT event will ordinarily arise when there is a change in ownership. This will ordinarily happen when you sell your property or gift it to your partner or children. Under the CGT provisions if you own a CGT asset (such as a rental property or holiday home) for more than 12 months; only half the capital gain is liable to tax at your marginal rates of tax. The balance is exempt and excluded from your assessable income. On the other hand if you sell a property within 12 months of buying it, the entire capital gain you make on disposal is liable to tax at your marginal rates. Incidentally, a CGT event arises at the time of the making of the contract rather than on the settlement date, when legal ownership normally changes hands (see chapter 4).

Main residence

Under Australian tax law your main residence is exempt from tax. This means you're not liable to pay any CGT if you make a capital gain on the sale of your home. The bad news is expenditure such as interest, council rates, insurance and repairs are not tax deductible. And if you make a capital loss you can't deduct it from a capital gain as the property is exempt from tax (see chapter 5).

Capital losses

Under Australian tax law if you make a capital loss on a sale, the capital loss can only be offset against a capital gain you make on the sale of other CGT assets that you own (such as shares and real estate). If you make no capital gains in the financial year that you incur a capital loss, the capital loss can be carried forward for an indefinite period, and can be offset against any future capital gains you derive. When a capital loss is offset against a capital gain you will effectively save paying tax on the capital gain you made. The tax you save will indirectly reduce the amount of the capital loss you incur (see chapter 4).

 Tax trap

Keep in mind you can only claim a 50 per cent CGT discount *after* you deduct all your current and prior year capital losses. For more details see chapter 4.

Useful references

- FIDO, the consumer website of the Australian Securities & Investments Commission <www.fido. gov.au> — go to 'Money tips', then 'Investing', then see 'Investing in real estate'.

- NSW fair trading <www.fairtrading.nsw.gov.au> —go to 'Tenants & Home Owners', then 'Being a landlord'.

- *Tax for Australians for Dummies* (John Wiley & Sons Australia Ltd).

Australian Taxation Office publications

- *Investment essentials*

- *Personal investor's guide to capital gains tax* (NAT 4152)

- *Private rulings and advice essentials*

- *Rental properties* (NAT 1729)

- *Rental properties—avoiding common mistakes*

- *Self-assessment and the taxpayer*

- *TaxPack* for individuals

- *TaxPack supplement* for individuals with investments

- *The compliance program—what is attracting our attention*

Chapter 2

Property speculator or property investor: why you need to know

In property transactions, the way you calculate your taxable income is primarily dependent on whether the Tax Office classifies you as carrying on a property business or as a property investor. When tax is involved, it's a black-and-white issue as to whether you are one or the other. Unfortunately you can't simply guess which camp you belong to, as tax penalties could apply if you get it wrong. In this chapter, I identify and explain how you're taxed if you carry on a property business or if you are a property investor, and the tests you will need to pass.

Defining who you are

Whether you're carrying on a property business or you're a property investor is a question of fact. If you're not sure it's best that you contact a recognised tax adviser (registered tax agent or legal practitioner) or seek a private ruling from the Tax Office. Whenever the terms 'carrying on a property business' or 'property investor' are used throughout this book they imply the following.

Carrying on a property business

Under this definition, you are carrying on business as a property developer/speculator (such as buying, building and renovating properties) with the predominant purpose of making a profit (and your properties are said to be held on 'revenue account'). If this is the case:

- You'll need to apply for an Australian Business Number (ABN) and quote this number whenever you enter into a commercial transaction. For more details see the Tax Office publication *ABN registration for individuals (sole traders)*.

- You'll need to register for goods and services tax (GST) and charge GST on your taxable sales. Under the GST provisions you're required to register if your annual GST turnover is likely to be $75 000 or more. If you are registered you can claim a GST credit for any GST you pay on business expenses (see chapter 3). For more details see the Tax Office publication *GST registration and carrying on an enterprise*.

- You'll need to prepare a business activity statement (BAS) each quarter disclosing information such as the total sales you derive less any GST credits you're entitled to claim back, and pay this amount to the Tax Office. To do this correctly you'll need to keep proper records of all your income and expenditure (especially your tax invoices) to substantiate any GST credits you intend to claim back.

- The properties you purchase are treated as trading stock on hand until they are sold. The costs associated with purchasing and renovating these properties will form part of the cost of trading stock on hand until they are sold. Incidentally, land can also constitute trading stock if you purchase land with the intention to resell it at a profit; see appendix A, Land and trading stock.

- At the end of each financial year you'll need to bring to account your trading stock on hand (namely, properties not yet sold) to calculate your taxable income. You can value your trading stock at cost price, market value or replacement value. Incidentally, 'taxable income' is defined as assessable income less allowable deductions, so you'll need to keep proper records for both sides of the equation.

- You can claim certain tax deductions commonly associated with carrying on a property business (for instance, contributions to a complying super fund are ordinarily tax-deductible expenses).

- The net profit you derive on the sale is the difference between the sale price and the costs you incur in buying, holding, renovating and selling the property.

- The net profit you derive is ordinarily recognised at the point of sale and more particularly on the settlement date; see appendix A, Derivation of income (sale of property—settlement date). It must be included as part of your assessable income. By contrast if you are a property investor, under the CGT (capital gains tax) provisions, your property is considered to have sold at the time the contract is made (see chapter 4).

- If you're carrying on a rental property business the accruals, or earning, basis may be the appropriate method for determining when rent is derived. Under this method rental income is treated as derived when you have a legal right to demand payment (such as when you issue an invoice). For more details see Tax Office Ruling TR 98/1, paragraph 48.

- Any trading losses you incur on a sale can be deducted from other assessable income you derive (for instance, from salary and wages, business profits and investment income such as interest, dividends and rent).

 Tax tip

If you own many rental properties (for instance, you manage and maintain a large block of flats) you may be considered to be carrying on a rental-property business. But if you own rental properties predominantly for the purposes of deriving rental income, you will not ordinarily be considered to be carrying on a property business; see appendix A, Maintenance of rental property (not carrying on a business).

Property investor

You're a property investor if the primary reason for buying an investment property is to derive rent; you don't need to apply for an ABN, nor quote this number to your tenant. Under the CGT provisions, your property holdings are treated as CGT assets. If this is the case:

- You'll need to apply for a Tax File Number (TFN) and quote this number whenever you contact the Tax Office or lodge your annual tax return disclosing the rental income you derive.

- You may need to prepare an Instalment Activity Statement disclosing the rent you derive and pay tax on a quarterly basis. The Tax Office will inform you whether you'll need to do this. This means you'll need to keep an accurate record of the gross rent you derive on an ongoing basis. Incidentally, rental expenses you incur are ignored when preparing this statement. For more details see the Tax Office publication *PAYG instalments—how to complete your activity statement.*

- Your property purchases are capital in nature and are not tax-deductible expenses. They will form part of the cost base and are taken into account to determine whether you have made a capital gain or capital loss on disposal (see chapter 4).

- The net rent you derive each year is treated as assessable income and is liable to tax when you receive the payment (see chapter 3).

- At the end of the financial year (30 June) you must prepare a profit and loss statement disclosing the net rent you derive (or net loss you incur), and disclose the amount in your annual tax return. To do this correctly you'll need to read the Tax Office publication *Business and professional items* and complete the 'Business and professional items schedule for individuals'.

- Any rent you derive must be disclosed at Item 21 in your tax return for individuals (supplementary section).

- Any capital gains and capital losses must be disclosed at Item 18: Capital gains, located in your tax return for individuals (supplementary section).

- You can only claim a tax deduction if a relevant connection exists between the expenditure you incur and the derivation of your rental income (see chapter 3).

- Profits and losses you make on the sale of your properties are considered under the CGT provisions. This means they will be classified as capital gains and capital losses and you will be taxed as follows:

  - A capital gain or capital loss is recognised at the time of the making of the contract, and not on the settlement date as is the case if you're carrying on a property business.

  - If you sell a property you've owned within 12 months of buying it, the entire capital gain is liable to tax.

  - If you sell a property you've owned for more than 12 months, only 50 per cent of the capital gain is liable to tax (see chapter 4).

  - If you make a capital loss you cannot deduct it from other assessable income you derive (for instance from salary and wages, business profits and investment income like rent). This is because you can only offset a capital loss from a capital gain (see chapter 4).

  - If you make no capital gains in the financial year that you make a capital loss, the capital loss is quarantined, and can be offset only against capital gains you may make in the future (for instance, from a capital gain on the sale of another property or shares).

Tax tip

The Tax Office has issued the publication *Are you in the business of renovating properties?* to explain the difference between the terms 'carrying on a property business' and 'property investor'. You can contact your local Tax Office or download a copy from the website <www.ato.gov.au>.

Carrying on a property business: the tests you need to pass

The Income Tax Assessment Act defines a 'business' for tax purposes as 'any profession, trade, employment, vocation or calling, but does not include occupation as an employee'. Whether you're carrying on a property business is a question of fact. The Tax Office uses a number of tests to determine whether you're carrying on a business of building or renovating properties to make a profit or whether you're a fair dinkum property investor. So effectively you can't guess. Under tax law it's a clear-cut decision—you're either one or the other. The key tests you'll need to consider are listed here.

- *Whether you intend to make a profit.* Your property transactions must be entered into for the purposes of making a profit.

- *Whether you're operating in a businesslike manner.* Your transactions must have a commercial flavour; for instance, you:

    □ have a business plan

- have access to immediate funds
- seek building approvals
- are in constant contact with professional property developers and/or real estate agents
- keep proper records of all the costs you incur
- have specific skills relating to the building industry and/or attend training courses
- are constantly on the lookout for potential properties to renovate.

- *The size and scale of your operations.* You must regularly buy, renovate and sell properties. As a rule of thumb the more you are engaged in these activities the greater the chance the Tax Office will classify you as carrying on a property business.

- *Whether you're operating to a set plan, budget or target.* For instance, you have:

  - set aside a certain amount of capital to bankroll your property transactions
  - a plan to make a certain amount of profit from each property transaction you enter into
  - specific plans/strategies in place as to when you should buy and sell property.

- *Whether you're maintaining proper records.* You must maintain accurate records of your purchases and sales. Your must properly account for your property activities (namely: sales – cost of goods sold – deductible expenses = net profit).

- *Whether you're trading on a full-time or part-time basis.* Under Australian tax law you can carry on a business in a small way, on either a full-time or part-time basis.

Although it's not necessary for you to satisfy every single test, the overall evidence (impression) must clearly indicate that your activities are similar to that of professional property developers or builders who ordinarily derive their income from buying, building and/or renovating properties for profit.

Case study: carrying on a property business

Mark, who is a school teacher, purchases an old, rundown residential property that he intends to renovate on weekends and during his annual holidays. Before he commences the project he attends a number of property seminars, seeks advice from a professional builder on some technical issues, and gets all the appropriate building approvals from the local council. His prime objective is to renovate and sell the property at a profit as soon as the project is completed (and if all goes according to plan to do it again in the future).

Although Mark is not a professional builder, under these circumstances it's likely that he is carrying on a business (or profit-making activity) renovating properties. This is because he enters into the project in a businesslike matter with the prime intention of renovating the property immediately and selling it at a profit. Any profit derived will be treated as assessable income.

Incidentally, if you enter into an isolated commercial transaction that's outside what you normally do for a living (as is the case here), any profit you make on sale is ordinarily treated as assessable income. This is on the proviso that the intention or purpose of entering into the transaction is to make a profit; see appendix A, Isolated transactions (profit motive).

 Tax trap

If you're on the borderline or you're not sure whether you're classified as carrying on a property business or as a property investor, don't guess. Tax penalties could apply if you get it wrong and you could find yourself paying more tax than is necessary. You should seek professional advice from a registered tax agent or get a private ruling from the Tax Office, as to whether your profits (or losses) should be taxed on revenue account or under the CGT provisions. If you plan to apply for a private ruling, the Tax Office has prepared the publication *Private rulings and advice essentials*. You can download a copy from the Tax Office website <www.ato.gov. au> and read the section 'Are you carrying on a business? (Supporting document requirements for private rulings)'. You'll need to address the key tests mentioned under 'Carrying on a property business: the tests you need to pass', as this will determine whether you're carrying on a property business or you're a genuine property investor.

Case study: property investor

Anita, who is a fashion designer, purchases a residential property with the prime intention of leasing it. To make the property more attractive to potential tenants she spends $30000 on repairs and renovations. On completion of these renovations, which she undertakes herself, the property is leased. When the lease expires three years later, Anita decides to sell the property and makes a $100000 profit on the sale.

Under these circumstances Anita is regarded as a property investor as her prime intention in purchasing the property is to lease it. The $30000 she spends on repairs and renovations is treated as 'initial repairs' and is not a tax-deductible expense (see chapter 3). However, these costs can be added to the property's cost base (see chapter 4). The $100000 profit on sale will be taxable under the CGT provisions. As the property has been owned for more than 12 months, only 50 per cent of the capital gain is liable to tax. The balance is exempt from tax and excluded from Anita's assessable income (see chapter 4).

At a glance: carrying on a property business versus property investor

Let's take a look at how you are taxed under Australian law:

Income

If you are a property builder/speculator, you will be aiming to make a quick profit from any property transaction you enter into. Holding a property to derive rent is not your motivating reason for purchasing the property. Instead, you will aim to buy a property, value add, and sell it immediately at an enhanced price. All proceeds from sale are treated as assessable income for tax purposes.

If you are a property investor, on the other hand, you will tend to hold your property mainly to derive a regular rental income, and benefit from long-term capital growth (rather than making a quick profit on sale). All rental income is assessable and any profit on a subsequent sale is treated as a capital gain under the CGT provisions.

Losses

A major benefit of being classified as carrying on a property business is that all trading losses and outgoings can be deducted from other assessable income you derive (for instance, from salary and wages, business profits and investment income). This will allow you to immediately recoup any trading losses and expenses you incur. So it's important that you have another source of income to offset your trading losses. Keep in mind that no tax is payable once your taxable income falls below $16 000 (per 2010–11 financial year), as you can claim a low income tax offset. So you could lose this significant benefit if your losses are substantial and your assessable income from other sources is minimal. Incidentally, business losses can be carried forward to the next financial year.

In contrast, if you're a property investor, any loss you incur is classified as a capital loss. Under the CGT provisions, a capital loss is quarantined and can only be offset against a capital gain.

Trading stock

If you carry on a property business, at the end of the financial year (30 June) you'll need to bring to account properties not yet sold as trading stock on hand. So you'll need to take into account the following:

- you can value your trading stock on hand at cost, market value or replacement value

- the closing value of your trading stock on hand on 30 June must be the same as the opening value of your trading stock at the beginning of the next financial year (namely 1 July).

On the other hand, if you're a property investor, you don't need to do this exercise because you're only required to bring to account your realised capital gains and capital losses.

Purchase costs

If you carry on a property business the total of your purchase costs is a tax-deductible expense. In contrast, if you're a property investor, your purchase costs (namely the purchase price plus incidental costs of purchase, such as stamp duty and legal costs) are capital in nature and form part of the property's cost base. These costs are taken into account to calculate whether you have made a capital gain or a capital loss on the sale of your property.

Deductible expenses

If you carry on a property business you can claim losses and outgoings incurred in gaining or producing assessable income or necessarily incurred in carrying on a business for the purposes of gaining or producing assessable income, such as rent and profits (see chapter 3).

In contrast, if you are a property investor, you can only claim losses and outgoings incurred in gaining or producing your rental income (see chapter 3).

CGT discount

A major limitation of being classified as carrying on a property business is that you can't claim a 50 per cent CGT discount for properties held for more than 12 months, as is the case if you're a property investor (see chapter 4).

CGT concessions for small business

If you carry on a property business and you sell an active asset that you use to run your business (for instance, your business premises, factory or yard), you could qualify for CGT relief under the CGT concessions for small business (see chapter 4). See also appendix A, Active asset (deriving rent).

Useful references

Most of the following resources can be found online.

Australian Taxation Office publications

- *Are you in the business of renovating properties?*

- *Are you carrying on a business?*

- *GST registration and carrying on an enterprise*

Australian Taxation Office interpretative decisions

- ID 2004/407: *Income tax: assessable income: residential properties instalment sales contracts — investor not carrying on a business*

Other taxation rulings

- IT 2450: *Income tax: recognition of income from long term construction contracts*

- TA 2009/5: *Use of an associate to obtain Goods and Services Tax (GST) benefits on construction of residential premises for lease*

CHAPTER 3

Taxing your property portfolio: the rules you need to follow

Under Australian taxation law the way your property transactions are taxed depends on whether you are carrying on a property business (such as a property developer/ property speculator) or you're a genuine property investor (see chapter 2). There are also numerous statutory tax rules and regulations associated with real estate that you'll need to comply with. So it's important that you understand what you're doing at the outset, as penalties could apply if you get it wrong. In this chapter I guide you through the key taxation principles associated with real estate.

At a glance: property and taxation

The following list provides a quick overview of how your property transactions are taxed. The meaty bits are discussed below.

- *Rent:* Rent is liable to tax when it's paid or credited to your account or to your real estate agent's account. You must also include any rent you receive from rental properties that you own overseas (see chapter 6).

- *Tax deductions:* Certain expenditure you incur in deriving your assessable income (rent) is tax deductible, but there must be a relevant connection between the two to qualify as a tax-deductible expense.

- *Construction costs:* You can write off the construction costs of income-producing buildings such as commercial premises and residential rental properties.

- *Trading profits and losses:* If you carry on a property business all your sales form part of your assessable income. The costs associated with purchasing and renovating properties will form part of the cost of trading stock on hand until they're sold. Your trading losses can be offset against other assessable income you derive (see chapter 2).

- *Capital gains and losses:* If you are a property investor you are liable to pay capital gains tax if you make a capital gain on sale, but only half the capital gain is taxable if you own a property for more than 12 months. A capital loss can only be offset against a capital gain.

- *Goods and services tax (GST):* A residential property used predominately for residential accommodation is input taxed. This means no GST is charged on the rent you collect from your tenant, and you can't claim a GST credit on expenditure you incur (for instance, the GST you pay on the agent's commission to collect the rent). Incidentally, the GST payable is a tax-deductible expense.

 Tax tip

If you carry on a rental-property business in which you're managing and maintaining a large number of rental properties, the income is ordinarily derived on an accruals basis (meaning when you have a legal right to demand payment), rather than when the rent is received, as is the case if you're a property investor (see chapter 2).

Rental income

The purpose of the Income Tax Assessment Act is to levy a tax on taxable income. Taxable income is defined as assessable income less allowable deductions. Included in the meaning of assessable income is income from property such as the rent you receive from leasing a commercial or residential property. Rent is a payment you get from a tenant for occupying your property over a given period of time. Under Australian tax law, if you're a property investor, rent is generally assessable when received or applied at the taxpayer's direction (per TR 98/1). This means any rent that's outstanding at the end of the financial year is not assessable until you receive the payment. Incidentally, if you derive rental income from leasing a residential property, you don't need to apply for an Australian Business Number (ABN), nor quote it to your tenant at the time you collect the rent. Furthermore, no GST is payable on rent you receive from residential property used predominately for residential accommodation.

 Tax trap

If you intend to lease a rental property to a relative (for instance, to your child), make sure you charge a commercial rate of rent. If you don't do this (for instance, you only charge $10 a week rent), there's a risk the Tax Office could reduce or disallow any rental expenditure you incur; see appendix A, Apportionment of rental deductions. For more details see TR IT 2167: *Income tax: rental properties—non-economic rental, holiday home, share of residence, etc. cases, family trust cases.*

If the rent you derive from your rental properties is likely to be substantial, you may need to prepare an 'Instalment

Activity Statement' and pay PAYG (pay-as-you-go) withholding tax on a quarterly basis. The Tax Office will inform you whether you'll need to do this, which means you'll have to keep track of the gross rent you receive at regular intervals. Incidentally, when preparing this statement the rental expenditure you incur each quarter is ignored, as the rate of tax payable takes into account the expenses you're likely to incur. The tax you pay each quarter is credited against your end of financial year assessment. For more information you can read the Tax Office publication *PAYG instalments—how to complete your activity statement (NAT 7392)*. You can get a copy from your local Tax Office or you can download a copy from its website <www.ato.gov.au>.

 Tax tip

If the rent you receive from a tenant is in the form of property (instead of a cash payment), you'll still need to declare it as part of your assessable income. Under these circumstances, you'll need to calculate its monetary value (for more details see ATO Interpretative Decision ID 2002/632).

At a glance: what's assessable

The following list provides examples of the types of receipts that are assessable:

- insurance payments you receive to compensate you for loss of rent

- letting or booking fees you receive for leasing your property

- cash lease incentives to enter into a lease to occupy business premises; see appendix A, Lease incentives

- prepaid rent at the time you receive it

- reimbursement for tax-deductible expenditure you incur (for instance, insurance claims)

- rental bond money you receive from a tenant when you have a legal right to keep it (for instance, when a tenant damages your property or defaults on the rent)

- rent you receive from an overseas rental property (see chapter 6).

At a glance: what's not assessable

The following list provides examples of what is not assessable.

- Payments received by family members for 'board and lodgings' are ordinarily considered to be in the nature of domestic arrangements and not assessable (for instance, children paying their parents for board and/or lodgings).

- Minimal amounts received from friends or relatives for staying at a holiday home that you own. The Tax Office considers these arrangements are 'in the nature of domestic and family arrangements', and the amounts received are reimbursements for costs incurred during the period of occupancy.

- Weekly instalments received for the sale of a residential property under an instalment contract; the payments are capital receipts (per ATO interpretative decision ATO ID 2003/968).

Claiming a tax deduction

A major pain with owning real estate is the never-ending inflow of expenses such as council rates, land taxes, water and sewage rates, insurance and repairs that you have to pay. This will be the case whether the property is leased or vacant. Under Australian tax law, for these types of expenses to be tax deductible there must be a relevant connection between the expenditure you incur and the derivation of your assessable income such as rent.

Technically speaking, the Income Tax Assessment Act points out that you can deduct from your assessable income any loss or outgoings to the extent that:

- it is incurred in gaining or producing assessable income (for instance, rent)

- it is necessarily incurred in carrying on a business for the purposes of gaining or producing assessable income (such as profits you derive from property speculation).

However you can't claim a loss or outgoing if it is capital, private or domestic in nature.

The Tax Office takes the view that if you derive rent from merely leasing rental properties that you own, you will not be considered to be carrying on a business (see chapter 2). This means if you're a property investor, you can only claim a tax deduction if there is a relevant connection between the expenditure you incur and the derivation of your rental income. For example, the payment of council rates and land taxes for your rental property has a relevant connection with deriving your rental income.

Incidentally, if your rental property becomes vacant (or it's being refurbished), you can still claim a tax deduction for any expenditure you incur. The fact that you're not receiving rent at the moment will not disqualify you from claiming a tax deduction, provided the property is 'genuinely available for rent' at a commercial rate; for example, it's listed with a real estate agent and/or you're advertising to find a suitable tenant.

On the other hand, if you're carrying on a property business (for instance, you are a property developer or speculator, or you manage and maintain a large block of flats), you can also claim certain losses or outgoings that are necessarily incurred in carrying on a property business, that are not ordinarily available to property investors (see Property business deductions on p. 45). But you can't claim a tax deduction if the expenditure is considered to be capital, private or domestic in nature.

Tax tip

If you lease your holiday home for a short period of time (for instance, during the school holidays), you can only claim a tax deduction during the period the property is genuinely available for rent. The tax deductions you can claim are ordinarily calculated on a time basis; see appendix A, Property (genuinely available for rent).

At a glance: what's tax deductible

The following list provides examples of the types of expenditure you can claim if you derive rental income:

- account-keeping fees for accounts held for investment purposes

- advertising costs to find a suitable tenant

- body corporate fees if you own a flat or apartment

- borrowing expenses (for more details see chapter 7)

- capital-works deductions (see Capital-works deductions on p. 59)

- the cost of defective building works reports (see ATO interpretative decision ID 2002/1027)

- the cost of evicting a tenant

- the cost of subscriptions to investment journals (provided it's for the purposes of deriving your rental income)

- council rates
- depreciation or decline in value (see Depreciation on p. 55)
- expenditure incurred in relation to the management of your rental property (for instance, the agent's commission to collect the rent, telephone calls, bookkeeping and postage)
- gardening and lawn mowing
- insurance on the building
- interest on borrowings used for the purposes of deriving your rental income (see chapter 7)
- internet access for managing your rental properties
- land tax
- land tax arrears (excluding any penalty component you incur); see ATO interpretative decision ID 2001/90
- legal expenses associated with preparing a lease and the discharge of it (see Legal expenses on p. 74)
- letting fees incurred prior to the property being available for rent; see ATO interpretative decision ID 2002/1096
- ongoing management fees or retainers paid to investment advisers for investment-related matters, but you can't claim a tax deduction for a fee paid for drawing up an initial investment plan
- pest-control expenses
- quantity-surveyor fees

- rates and other holding expenses on vacant land held for future income-producing purposes; see ATO interpretative decision ID 2001/479

- rental fee for a safe deposit box to safeguard your investment-related securities; for instance, documents like your certificate of title

- repairs and maintenance (see Repairs on p. 48)

- security-patrol fees

- tax-agent fees for managing your tax affairs and lodging your individual tax return

- travel expenses to inspect your investment properties and collect the rent

- water and sewage charges.

 Tax tip

Giving away land you own with a market value of more than $5000 to an eligible environmental body for a conservation purpose may qualify for an income-tax deduction. For more details see the Tax Office publication *Conservation covenant concessions*.

 Tax tip

If you own rental properties and you attend a property-investment seminar or workshop that directly relates to deriving rental income from your

Tax tip *(cont'd)*

existing rental properties, the expenses you incur in attending (such as airfares, accommodation and fees) are ordinarily a tax-deductible expense. For more details see ATO interpretative decision ID 2003/324 *Income tax: Deductions: rental property expenses: property investment seminar.*

At a glance: what's not tax deductible

If you derive rental income you can't claim:

- bond money paid to lease a rental property used to operate a business activity

- costs associated with purchasing a rental property, as the expenditure is considered to be capital in nature (they form part of establishing an income-producing asset)

- land tax paid on property no longer producing income

- costs associated with setting up a rental property

- certain repairs (such as replacement of kitchen cupboards in a rental property)

- expenditure incurred in underpinning the foundations of a rental property

- costs associated with hiring a property buyer's agent to purchase a rental property

- costs incurred in relocating assets (for instance, a refrigerator and washing machine) from a previous rental property to a new rental property

- security devices installed in your main residence to protect you and your family (for instance, alarms, security locks to windows and external lighting); see appendix A, Security costs (Security locks & external lighting installed in family home).

 Tax tip

There are special tax rules for claiming any prepaid rental expenses you incur, such as interest payments and insurance. To qualify for an immediate tax deduction the eligible service period (to which the prepaid expense relates) must be 12 months or less, and must end on or before the end of the financial year (30 June). If this is not the case and your prepaid expense is $1000 or more, you'll need to spread the prepaid expense over two or more financial years. For more details see the Tax Office publication *Deductions for prepaid expenses (NAT 4170)*. You can download a copy from the Tax Office website.

Property business deductions

If you carry on a property business (as a property developer or speculator), then you can claim the following tax deductions as they are considered to be necessarily incurred in carrying on a business:

- the purchase price of properties. This is because they are regarded as trading stock (see chapter 2). Note the capital gains tax (CGT) provisions do not apply to properties held as trading stock. This means you can't claim a 50 per cent CGT discount on properties held for more than 12 months (see chapter 4). Costs of unsold properties will be treated a trading stock on hand.

- costs associated with renovating properties.

- agent's commission and GST you incur in selling properties.

- costs of maintaining an office.

- interest on borrowings to buy properties and, more particularly, your trading stock (see chapter 7).

- contributions to a complying super fund (provided the contributions do not exceed a statutory cap amount).

Trading losses can be deducted from other assessable income you derive (such as salary and wages, business profits and investment income).

 Tax tip

If you're planning on building a rental property, expenditure such as interest payments, local council rates, water and sewage rates, land taxes and levies for emergency services, which you may incur while the property is under construction, are tax deductible. This is on the condition that the property will be constructed within a reasonable period of time, and that it will be used to derive assessable income (rent).

Specific deductions relating to property

There are statutory rules you'll need to satisfy if you want to claim the following tax-deductible expenses relating to rental properties:

- legal expenses

- repairs

- depreciation (decline in value)

- capital-works deductions.

Legal expenses

If you're a property investor or you carry on a property business you may need to seek legal advice from time to time about a particular matter. Under Australian tax law legal costs are tax-deductible expenses if they have a relevant connection with the derivation of your rental income, or they are necessarily incurred in carrying on a property business for the purposes of deriving assessable income.

At a glance: what's tax deductible

Ordinarily you can claim a tax deduction for legal expenses incurred in:

- complying with the Income Tax Assessment Act

- preparing a lease agreement with a tenant

- securing a loan to buy a rental property (see chapter 7)

- discharging a mortgage

- defending a claim for damages for injuries allegedly suffered by a person visiting a tenant at your rental property

- taking court action to recover lost rental income

- evicting a tenant who refuses to pay you rent.

At a glance: what's not tax deductible

If you're a property investor, you can't claim legal costs associated with buying and selling a rental property. These costs are added to the property's cost base and are taken into account when calculating a capital gain or capital loss on the sale of your property (see chapter 4).

Repairs

Landlords have a legal obligation to undertake necessary repairs and maintenance and attend to requests from tenants to remedy any urgent defects (see chapter 1). Under Australian tax law, there are strict rules relating to claiming repairs as a tax deduction. It's not a simple matter of ringing up someone to come and fix the problem. This is because if you do more than merely repair the item, the expenditure is capital in nature and not tax deductible as a repair, and there's often a fine line between the two.

To help you to comply with the statutory rules, the Tax Office has issued guidelines on what is considered a repair for the purposes of the Tax Act. So if you're planning on doing some major renovations or repairs to your property, it's best to seek advice from a recognised tax adviser on what you can and can't claim *before you start*. It can be a bit of a minefield (and costly!) to work out what is tax deductible after the event. It may be worthwhile taking photographs while you're renovating or repairing the property.

Expressed simply, a repair is the replacement of worn-out parts with new parts, in order to restore the item being repaired to its former level of efficiency. According to the Tax Office, 'a repair for the most part is occasional and partial. It involves restoration of efficiency of function of the property being repaired without changing its character, and may include restoration to its former appearance, form, state or condition' (per Tax Office Ruling TR 97/23).

At a glance: what's tax deductible

The following are examples of repairs:

- electrical repairs
- general maintenance and upkeep

- plumbing repairs

- removing worn carpets and polishing existing floorboards in a rental property

- repainting faded walls

- repairing a leaking roof

- repairing broken doors and windows.

At a glance: what's not tax deductible

The Tax Office does not consider the following examples of work on a rental property to be repairs:

- rebuilding the external protective wall

- replacing kitchen cupboards

- underpinning the foundations.

 Tax trap

Under Australian tax law a repair is not tax deductible if the expenditure is capital in nature. It must not be:

⇒ a repair undertaken to the entirety

⇒ an improvement

⇒ an initial repair.

A repair undertaken to the entirety

If you plan to repair an item make sure you restore it to its previous condition by simply replacing any worn-out parts with new parts. Don't improve its efficiency or change its character along the way. If you do, the expenditure may be capital in nature and not tax deductible.

For example, if you replace a couple of rusted galvanised roof sheets with new ones the expenditure is clearly a repair, as you're merely replacing some worn-out parts with new parts, and restoring the efficiency of function of the galvanised roof. But if you decide to replace the entire galvanised roof with terracotta tiles that are more efficient and durable, the expenditure is capital in nature and not tax deductible. This is because you have effectively replaced 'its entirety' and changed its original character — the roof is no longer a galvanised roof but rather a more efficient terracotta roof. Incidentally, under Australian tax law, the term 'entirety' is defined as something separately identifiable as a principal item of capital equipment, maintaining its own function. But the good news here is that if you can't claim the expenditure as a repair, you can claim it under the capital-works deductions provisions (see Capital-works deductions on p. 59).

 Tax tip

If you repair a rental property that has become vacant, the expenses you incur could qualify as a

Tax tip *(cont'd)*

tax-deductible expense. This is also the case if you repair business premises after income production has ceased. But this is on the condition that the repairs arise as a result of you using the property to derive assessable income. For more details, see Tax Ruling IT 180.

Improvements

Under Australian tax law a deduction for repairs will not be allowed if they result in an *improvement* that:

- changes the character of the item being repaired

- reduces the likelihood of future repairs

- increases or adds some additional functions to the item you're repairing

- enhances the operation of the item you're repairing.

For example, you decide to replace a rotten wooden floor with a better, long-lasting and more moisture-resistant concrete floor. Although you may have solved the problem at hand, according to judicial authority if you plan to do this, the expenditure will be considered an improvement and is not deductible as a repair. If you find you can't claim the expense as a repair, you may qualify for a tax deduction under the capital-works provisions (see Capital-works deductions on p. 59).

Tax tip

Using different materials to repair an item does not necessarily prevent you from claiming a repair, provided it merely restores the efficiency of the previous function without changing its character. But if different materials produce a new or additional function, the expenditure will be considered capital in nature and not tax deductible as a repair. If in doubt you should seek professional advice.

Tax trap

The Tax Office has issued a ruling pointing out that 'If work done goes beyond "repair" and the whole cost is capital expenditure', you cannot claim a tax deduction for *notional repairs*, 'i.e., an amount it is estimated that repair work would have cost the taxpayer if the property had in fact merely been repaired'.

Initial repairs

There is a well-established principle in tax law that you can't claim 'initial repairs' as a tax-deductible expense; see appendix A, Repairs. This is a common mistake that the Tax Office will quickly pounce on if you were to be audited! (See chapter 9.) Technically speaking, 'initial repairs' are repairs you make to a newly acquired property that were required at the time you purchased the property, the logic being that you effectively paid less for the property as a result of these existing defects.

For example, at the time you purchase a rental property you decide to spend $25 000 replacing the property's rusted spouting and repainting all the faded walls to make it more appealing to a prospective tenant. Although this may seem like a smart move, unfortunately under Australian tax law, the expenditure is considered to be capital in nature and not tax deductible. This is because the need to do these repairs did not arise during the time you owned and used the property to derive assessable income. These repairs arose as a consequence of the previous owner's use of the property.

But there is some good news. Although you can't claim the expense as a repair, you may qualify for a tax deduction under the capital-works provisions (see Capital-works deductions on p. 59).

 Tax tip

If you incur travel and accommodation costs to carry out initial repairs on a rental property in order to make it more attractive to potential tenants, the costs can be added to the property's cost base (and, more particularly, the third element of the cost base). This is also the case if you own a holiday home (see chapter 4).

Depreciation

When you buy an income-producing property such as your business premises or rental property, the first thing you should do is inspect the property with a fine-toothed comb, and make a list of every item that qualifies as a depreciating asset. To help you identify what items are depreciable, the Tax Office has published a comprehensive list of depreciable items in its publication *Rental properties (NAT 1729)*; you can get a copy from its website. Examples of some of the items you can depreciate are listed on p. 57.

Tax tip

Qualified quantity surveyors can value items that qualify for a depreciation deduction. They can also help you compile a schedule of items you can depreciate, and items you can claim under the capital-works deductions provisions. The fees they charge are ordinarily tax-deductible expenses.

Technically speaking, depreciation (or decline in value as the Tax Office would rather call it) is claiming a tax deduction for wear and tear of depreciable items that you have installed and use to derive your rental income.

Under Australian tax law there are two ways you can claim a depreciation deduction — the prime cost method (PCM) and diminishing value method (DVM). The first method allows you to claim a fixed amount each year until the item is written off. The second method allows you to claim a bigger amount in the earlier years and a smaller amount in later years. When tossing up which method to use, keep in mind that the rate of depreciation under DVM is twice the rate under PCM. So if the rate of depreciation under PCM is 20 per cent, under DVM it is automatically 40 per cent. Incidentally, if the cost of a depreciable item you use to derive rental income is $300 or less, you can claim an immediate tax deduction.

The Tax Act allows you to estimate the depreciable item's effective life when you're working out an appropriate rate of depreciation. For example, if you estimate the effective life of a gas stove to be five years, the rate of depreciation is 20 per cent under PCM (or 40 per cent if you elect to use DVM). Alternatively, if you don't want to estimate the effective life, the Tax Office publishes each year the depreciation rates of a number of items relating to rental properties (see the Tax Office publication *Rental property*).

Unfortunately there are certain items that you can't depreciate for tax purposes (see At a glance: What you can't depreciate on p. 58). Incidentally, if you sell (or scrap) a depreciable item for less than the item's adjusted value (or written-down value), the loss you incur (referred to as the balancing adjustment amount) is a tax-deductible expense. On the other hand, if you sell it for more than the adjusted value, the balancing adjustment amount can be taxed and must be included as part of your assessable income.

At a glance: what you can depreciate

The following items typically found in a residential rental property are examples of items you can depreciate:

- air-conditioning assets

- alarms

- clothes dryers

- cooktops

- crockery and cutlery

- dishwashers

- floor coverings (carpets, linoleum, vinyl)

- freezers

- furniture

- heaters

- hot-water systems

- linen

- solar-power-generating system assets

- stoves

- television sets

- washing machines.

At a glance: what you can't depreciate

The following items typically found in a residential rental property are examples of items you can't depreciate:

- built-in wardrobes
- carports
- clothes lines
- electrical wiring
- kitchen cupboards
- laundry fixtures
- letterboxes
- saunas (excluding heating assets)
- spa baths (excluding pumps)
- swimming pools
- television antennas, fixed
- ventilation ducting and vents
- water tanks.

Note: these expenses may be deductible under the capital-works deductions provisions (see Capital-works deductions for more details).

 Tax tip

There is a special method called 'low value pools' that you can use to combine depreciable items that cost between $301 and $1000. This method allows you to use the DVM and you can depreciate these items at the rate of 37.5 per cent. For more details see the Tax Office publication *Guide to depreciating assets*.

Capital-works deductions

Under the capital-works deductions provisions, you can write off the construction costs of certain items that don't qualify for a depreciation deduction, and the construction costs of income-producing buildings (such as office space, shops, factories and residential rental properties). Depending on when the non-depreciable items were first installed or the buildings first constructed, you can write them off over a period of 25 or 40 years (see table 3.1).

Table 3.1: key construction dates

Date construction commenced	Annual deduction rate
22 August 1979 to 21 August 1984	2.5 per cent
22 August 1984 to 15 September 1987	4 per cent
After 15 September 1987	2.5 per cent

At a glance: capital-works deductions for non-depreciable items

The types of non-depreciable items normally found in a residential rental property that you can claim under the capital-works deductions provisions include:

- automatic garage doors (excluding controls and motors)

- built-in wardrobes

- fencing

- garden sheds, other than freestanding

- gates (excluding electrical controls and motors)

- kitchen fixtures (such as benchtops, cupboards, sinks, taps and tiles)

- laundry fixtures (such as taps, tiles and tubs)

- letterboxes

- retaining walls

- spa baths (excluding pumps)

- swimming pools

- water tanks.

Capital-works deductions and buildings

If you buy a new property that you intend to lease, the amount you can write off each year is calculated with reference to the building's construction costs, and *not the price you paid* for the property. For example, if the purchase price is $800 000 and the building's construction costs are $400 000, you can only write off

$400 000 over a 25- or 40-year period. Incidentally, you can claim capital-works deductions if you make 'initial repairs' to a newly acquired property (see Repairs on p. 48).

 Tax tip

If you buy an existing property any capital-works deductions not yet claimed can be passed on to you. At the time of purchase you'll need to know when the property was first built and the construction costs that qualify for a tax deduction. If the construction costs are unknown you can get an estimate from a qualified person (such as a quantity surveyor).

At a glance: what construction costs are in

You can claim construction costs for:

- buildings (such as commercial and residential buildings)

- extensions (for instance, you add an extra room or build a garage)

- alterations or improvements to buildings that are not deductible as repairs

- structural improvements (for instance, a carport, sealed driveway, retaining wall or fence).

At a glance: what construction costs are out

The following expenditure cannot be included as part of the construction costs:

- the cost of the land

- clearing the land prior to construction

- landscaping

- the value of the owner/builder's contributions to the works (such as labour and expertise).

 Tax tip

Under the capital-works deductions provisions, construction expenditure can include architect fees, engineering fees, foundation excavation expenses, the cost of building permits and consultant fees. For more information see Tax Office Ruling TR 97/25.

 Tax trap

The Tax Office has drawn attention to two common mistakes—incorrectly claiming capital-works deductions that exceed the construction expenditure, and incorrectly claiming the cost of the land as a capital-works deduction (see chapter 9).

Capital-works deductions: the rules you need to follow

Technically speaking, you can't claim capital-works deductions until the construction is completed and the property is rented or is available for rent. Furthermore, you can only claim a deduction for buildings that were constructed after a certain date (see table 3.1 on p. 59). If a residential rental property is constructed after 15 September 1987, you can claim a 2.5 per cent per annum tax deduction over a 40-year period.

For example, you buy a new residential property and the builder advises you that the construction costs that qualify for capital-works deductions are $400 000. Under these circumstances (provided the property is rented or available for rent) you can claim a $10 000 deduction each year for the next 40 years ($400 000 × 2.5 per cent = $10 000). But the sting in the tail is that the amount you claim each year (in this example $10 000) must be deducted from the property's cost base. This nasty rule applies to income-producing properties purchased after 13 May 1997.

Case study: reducing the cost base

Ten years ago Charlie paid $800 000 for a new residential property that he intended to lease. At the time of purchase, the builder advised him that the construction expenditure that qualified for a tax deduction under the capital-works provisions was $400000. As the building was constructed after 1987 and is used to derive rental income, Charlie could claim a $10000 tax deduction for the next 40 years ($400000 × 2.5 per cent = $10000). Charlie sold the property today and received $1.2 million. Over the period he owned the property the total amount of capital-works deductions Charlie claimed amounted to $100000 ($10000 × 10 years). As Charlie purchased the property after 13 May 1997, he needs to reduce the property's cost base by $100000, to calculate the amount of his capital gain that's liable to tax. Incidentally, when Charlie sells the property, the amount of capital works not yet written off can be claimed by the new owner, provided the property is used to derive assessable income.

Capital proceeds (sale price)		$1200000
Less:		
Cost base:		
Purchase price	$800000	
Less:		
Capital-works deductions	$100000	$700000
Net capital gain		$500000

As Charlie owned the property for more than 12 months, he's only liable to pay tax on half the net capital gain he made on sale (namely $250000). See chapter 4 for more details.

Goods and services tax

The goods and services tax (GST) is a broad-based tax of 10 per cent on most goods and services that are sold or consumed in Australia. It first began to operate in Australia on 1 July 2000. Under the GST provisions you are likely to enter into three types of GST transactions. They are referred to as:

- *taxable sales* (for instance, you buy a newly constructed property or a property that has been substantially renovated from a professional builder)

- *input taxed sales* (for instance, you lease a residential property used predominantly for residential accommodation)

- *GST-free sales* (such as council rates).

For a property transaction you're generally liable to pay GST if you buy a new property (or one that has been substantially renovated) from a registered entity such as a builder.

If you lease a commercial property (for instance, an office or shop) you may need to register for GST. This will be the case if your annual GST turnover is likely to be $75 000 or more. You can also voluntarily register for GST if your GST turnover is less than $75 000. If you are registered (or required to be registered) you'll need to collect GST from your tenant for the rent you charge. But the good news here is that you can claim a GST credit for any GST you incur on your own acquisitions (for instance, GST payable on repairs, or on agent's commission to collect the rent on your behalf). This is also the case if you buy a commercial property.

But there is some paper work you'll need to attend to. You'll need to prepare a business activity statement (BAS) and calculate the amount of GST you collect from your tenant, less any GST you can claim back. This amount must be forwarded to the Tax Office, normally on a quarterly basis (see figure 3.1).

On the other hand, if you lease a residential property used predominantly for residential accommodation, the transaction is classified as an 'input taxed sale'. This means you cannot charge your tenant GST on the rent you receive, and you cannot claim a GST credit for any GST you pay (for instance, GST paid on repairs or on an agent's commission to collect the rent on your behalf). This is also the case if you buy or sell an existing (previously built) residential property (see figure 3.1). The Tax Office has published a booklet called *GST and property (NAT 72957),* which explains how GST applies to property sales and transactions. You can download a copy from the Tax Office website <www.ato.gov.au>.

At a glance: GST and property

GST applies to the following transactions:

- new property sold by registered entities (for instance, builders/property developers)
- property that had been substantially renovated (substantial improvement/makeover)
- sale of commercial properties
- rent collected from commercial tenants
- agent's commission to collect the rent
- repairs and renovations.

Figure 3.1: GST and property

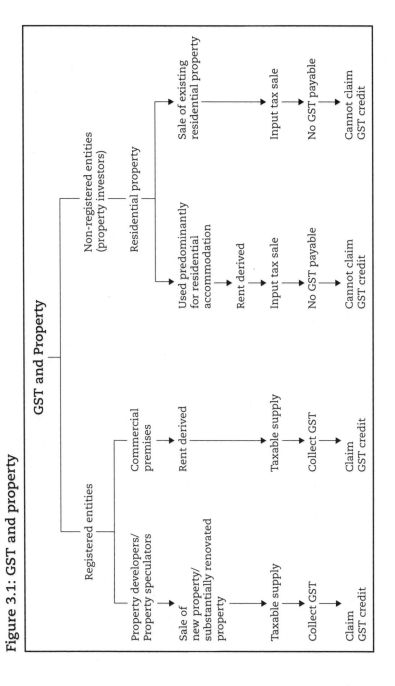

GST does not apply to the following transactions:

- rent collected from residential property used predominantly for residential accommodation

- sale of existing residential property

- council rates, water and sewerage

- unregistered entities building their main residence.

 Tax tip

Special rules apply if you carry on a business as a sole trader or partnership and you incur business losses. Under the non-commercial losses provisions if you don't satisfy certain conditions, you cannot deduct your business losses from other assessable income you may derive (such as salary and wages). These losses can only be deducted from business profits you make in future years. However, this provision will not apply if you have real property (such as land and buildings) worth at least $500 000 in the business on a continuing basis. For more details see the Tax Office publication *Non-commercial losses: overview—fact sheet.*

Useful references

Australian Taxation Office publications

- *Deductions for prepaid expenses (NAT 4170)*

- *Guide to depreciating assets (NAT 1996)*

- *Rental expenses—claiming capital works deductions (NAT 72840)*

- *Rental properties—claiming legal expenses (NAT 71956)*

- *Rental properties—claiming repairs and maintenance (NAT 72841)*

- *Rental property deductions—know what you can claim*

- *Valuations for the margin scheme (NAT 73397)*

Australian Taxation Office interpretative decisions

- ID 2002/170: *Income tax: deductibility of legal expenses—Breaches of management contract over a rental property*

- ID 2002/1098: *Income tax: consultants fee in relation to building an investment property*

- ID 2003/526: *Income tax: assessability of lump sum payment—for life time right to reside in a property—rent in advance*

Other taxation rulings

- TR 97/23: *Income tax: deduction for repairs*

- TD 98/19: *Income tax: capital gains: may initial repair expenditure incurred after the acquisition of a CGT asset be included in the relevant cost base of the asset?*

- GSTD 2000/9: *Goods and Services Tax: if you let out a residence do you need to get an ABN for PAYG purposes or register for GST?*

CHAPTER 4

Taxing your capital gains: sharing your good fortune

Australia introduced a capital gains tax (CGT) on 19 September 1985. Its prime objective is to tax the capital gains you make on the disposal of CGT assets (such as commercial and residential properties) that you have acquired since 20 September 1985. One exception to the rule is your main residence—it is exempt from tax (which is good to know if property values are going through the roof!—see chapter 5). For assets, and more particularly real estate purchased before 20 September 1985, no CGT is payable if you make a capital gain on sale. Great news if you're likely to make a capital gain; but not so great if it turns out you're likely to incur a capital loss, as the capital loss cannot be used! On 21 September 1999 the federal government changed the method of calculating the amount of any capital gain you make that's liable to tax (see figure 4.1 on p. 76). In this chapter, I discuss the impact of the CGT provisions on your property transactions and explain how you're taxed.

Back in the good old days

Prior to the introduction of the CGT provisions you were automatically taxed if you made a profit on the sale of a property you bought and sold within 12 months. You were also liable to pay tax if the main reason for buying a property was for a profit-making purpose (for instance, you were a property developer/property speculator carrying on a business of buying and selling property with a view to making a profit). So if you were a property investor back in the good old days, you would have been laughing all the way to the bank. This was because any profit on the sale of a rental property would not have been taxable. But if you had made a loss on the sale, the onus was on you to prove to the Tax Office that your prime motivation in buying the rental property in the first place was for a profit-making purpose. Trying to prove this back then was equivalent to trying to extract blood from a stone, which meant that you couldn't claim the loss as a tax deduction!

With the introduction of the CGT provisions, the grey area around whether a profit or loss is assessable or deductible has been removed. In other words, if the profit is not assessable (or the loss is not deductible), for instance, because you're not carrying on a property business, it will immediately fall for consideration under the CGT provisions. So no matter what your situation is you're going to be taxed one way or the other!

 Tax tip

If you construct a building on land you acquired before 20 September 1985, the building will be treated as a separate asset under the CGT provisions. This means if you sell the property at a later date only the building is liable to CGT, as the land will be treated as a 'pre-CGT asset'.

At a glance: CGT and property

This is how the CGT provisions work for property transactions.

- For a CGT liability to arise there must be a CGT event. This will normally happen when there is a 'disposal' of a CGT asset. This will ordinarily occur when there is a change in ownership, such as when you sell a property or gift it to someone. It can also arise if your property is destroyed.

- If you buy and sell a property within 12 months and you make a capital gain, the entire amount you make on the sale is liable to tax.

- If you sell a property 12 months after you buy it and you make a capital gain, only 50 per cent of the capital gain is taxable.

- Your main residence is exempt from tax. This is on the condition that it's not used to derive assessable income. But a partial exemption will apply if you use part of your main residence to derive assessable income (see chapter 5).

- If you operate a small business and you sell your business premises or transfer it to your self-managed super fund, under the CGT concessions for small business, the capital gain you make on disposal may be concessionally taxed or exempt from tax (see chapter 8).

- Profits and losses on the sale of properties purchased before the 20 September 1985 are excluded from the CGT provisions.

- The rules for calculating a capital gain changed on 21 September 1999 (see figure 4.1 on p. 76).

- If you make a capital loss on the sale of a CGT asset (property), the capital loss can only be deducted from a current or future capital gain you make on the sale of another CGT asset (such as real estate and/or shares).

- If you own a property in your self managed superannuation fund, no CGT is payable if your super fund is in the pension phase, and you sell the property after you turn 60 years of age and retire (see chapter 8).

- Under the CGT provisions a building is not a separate asset from the land.

Tax trap

If you give or transfer a property to someone (for instance, to your child) for nil consideration (nothing), under the CGT provisions you will be deemed to have sold the property at its market value. You will be liable to pay CGT if you would have made a capital gain (or you can claim a capital loss) at the time of disposal. Incidentally, the person you give the property to will be personally liable to pay state stamp duty for the kind gesture you're made!

Under the CGT provisions, you're liable to pay tax if the sale price (capital proceeds) you receive on sale is greater than the property's cost base. The term cost base means cost price plus certain costs you incur such as stamp duty, legal fees and agent's commission. When the CGT provisions were first introduced back in 1985, if you owned a CGT asset (such as real estate) for more than 12 months, you were permitted to adjust the capital gain for inflation. This was done by adjusting the property's cost base. The consumer price index is used to make this adjustment. This is the index that measures Australia's rate of inflation (see table 4.1 and more particularly the section Property bought between 20 September 1985 and 21 September 1999 on p. 85).

On 21 September 1999 the federal government changed the rules for calculating a capital gain. The way you calculate a capital gain today depends on whether you purchased a CGT asset (such as real estate) before or after 21 September 1999.

Figure 4.1: CGT and property

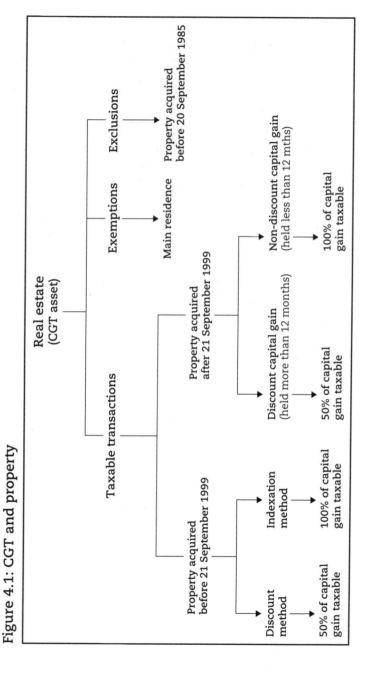

Tax tip

If you make capital improvements to a property you acquired before 20 September 1985, under the CGT provisions, the capital improvements may be treated as a separate CGT asset and may be liable to CGT on disposal. However, this will only apply if the cost of the capital improvements is more than 5 per cent of the amount you receive when you sell the dwelling, and greater than an 'improvement threshold', which is adjusted annually for inflation. For example, for the financial year ended 30 June 2011 the improvement threshold was set at $126 619. For more details you can read the Tax Office publication *Major capital improvements to a dwelling*. You can download a copy from the Tax Office website <www.ato.gov.au>.

How a capital gain is calculated

Under the CGT provisions, you will be considered to have made a capital gain if the 'capital proceeds' (sale price) is greater than the property's 'cost base'. The formula to calculate a capital gain is 'capital proceeds − cost base = capital gain'.

The capital proceeds can be a cash payment (which is normally the case) plus the market value of any items you receive (for instance, if you are paid in cash plus a 1951 fully restored Ferrari). The cost base is made up of a combination of five elements:

- *The property's 'purchase price'.* As set out in the contract of sale.

- *The 'incidental costs' associated with buying and selling a property.* This can include costs such as stamp duty, title search fees, valuation fees, conveyancing costs, accounting fees, the agent's commission to sell the property and the cost of advertising or marketing to find a buyer.

- *The non-deductible holding costs.* If you own a property that you use for your personal use and enjoyment (for instance, a holiday home), you can include in the cost base expenditure such as interest payments on a loan to buy the property, council rates and land taxes, insurance and repairs that don't qualify as a tax deduction (see Non-deductible holding costs on p. 93). Remember, you can only claim a tax deduction if the property is used to derive assessable income such as rent (see chapter 3).

- *The capital improvements you make to your property.* For instance, if you modernise the kitchen and bathroom or add extra rooms to the property.

- *The capital costs to preserve or defend the title or right to your property.* For instance, if you take legal action to stop someone from illegally entering your property and building a dwelling on your block of land.

To substantiate the cost base, it's quite obvious that you need to maintain accurate records to verify the costs you incur over the years. Trying to collate the different bits and pieces that make up the cost base can be a bit of a nightmare. This is especially the case if you inherit a holiday home for which no records were kept. So it's best to maintain a file of the various costs that make up the cost base. It'll save you a lot of money and heartache in the long term and it can be expensive to get a tax agent to do it on your behalf (see chapter 9).

At a glance: cost base—what's in

The Tax Office has provided examples of the types of costs that can be included as part of the cost base of a property:

- travel and accommodation costs incurred to carry out 'initial repairs' to a newly acquired rental property; they're included in the third element of the cost base (see chapter 3 for a discussion about initial repairs).

- travel costs incurred to carry out maintenance on a non-income-producing property such as a holiday home; they're included in the third element of the cost base.

- consultant fees to find and recommend a suitable rental property, provided you later purchase the property; they're included in the second element of the cost base.

- any underground power levy incurred by the owner of a rental property for putting overhead electric power lines underground; they're included in the fourth element of the cost base.

- cost of pest and building inspections, provided you later purchase the property; they're included in the second element of the cost base.

At a glance: cost base—what's out

The Tax Office has provided examples of the types of costs that can't be included as part of the cost base of a property:

- goods and services tax credits. If you're registered for GST (for example, if you are a property developer or speculator), you'll need to reduce the various elements of the property's cost base by any related GST credits you are entitled to claim back (see chapter 3).

- claimed capital works deductions. For property purchased after 13 May 1987, you'll need to reduce the cost base by the amount of any capital works deductions you had previously claimed as a tax-deductible expense (see chapter 3).

- entertainment expenses associated with selling a property.

For a comprehensive list of the types of specific expenditure that can be included in the cost base, see the Tax Office publication *Guide to capital gains tax*, particularly the section that deals with 'Elements of the cost base'. You can download a copy from the Tax Office website <www.ato.gov.au>.

Property bought after 21 September 1999

If you bought a property after 21 September 1999 or, more particularly, you buy one today, and you make a capital gain on the sale, calculating a capital gain is relatively straightforward. There are two rules you need to know:

- If you sell a property within 12 months of buying it and you make a capital gain, the entire amount is taxable. The Tax Office calls this capital gain a 'non-discount capital gain' to indicate that this specific capital gain you made on disposal is taxable in full. Incidentally, this rule is consistent with the same 12-months ownership rule that was in place before the CGT provisions were introduced back in 1985 and before 21 September 1999.

- If you sell a property at least 12 months after you buy it and you make a capital gain, only 50 per cent of the capital gain is taxable. The balance is exempt. The Tax Office calls this capital gain 'a discount capital gain' to indicate that only 50 per cent of this specific capital gain you made on disposal is taxable. So there is an incentive here for you to keep CGT assets (such as property and shares that have the capacity to appreciate in value) for at least 12 months.

Under the CGT provisions, you will be considered to have sold your property at the time the contract is made, rather than on the settlement date, which is when legal ownership ordinarily transfers to the new owner. For example, if you enter into a contract of sale on 1 June 2012 and the settlement date is 1 August 2012, under the CGT provisions, you will be considered to have sold the property on 1 June 2012. Any capital gain you make on sale is liable to tax in the financial year the contract of sale was entered into. In the above example, you'll need to declare the capital gain in the 2011–12 financial year rather than the 2012–13 financial year when legal ownership is transferred to the purchaser. Incidentally, the Tax Office has indicated that this is a common mistake when calculating a capital gain or capital loss (see chapter 9). The date you enter into the contract of sale is also used to determine whether you'll qualify for a 50 per cent CGT discount.

 Tax trap

If you are an Australian resident and you make a capital gain on the sale of a property you own overseas, you'll need to include the amount as part of the assessable income you derive in Australia. The capital gain is calculated in the same way you calculate a capital gain if you sell a property in Australia. This will be the case even if you have to pay foreign tax on the capital gain you made overseas. If foreign tax is payable you can claim a foreign income tax offset (see chapter 6).

Case study: property bought after 21 September 1999

Seven years ago Hannah paid $350000 for a property that she then leased. The incidental costs associated with the purchase were $12000 for stamp duty and $1000 for legal fees. Hannah sells the property today for $750000. The incidental costs associated with selling the property are $18000 for the agent's commission, $2000 for advertising and $1000 for legal fees. Three years prior to selling the property Hannah paid $50000 to modernise the kitchen and bathroom. During the period of time Hannah owned the property, she paid $120000 interest on borrowings to purchase the property, council rates and land taxes, insurance and repairs, which were all tax-deductible expenses.

As Hannah purchased the property after 21 September 1999 and owned it for more than 12 months, only 50 per cent of the capital gain she made on the sale is taxable. The balance is exempt and excluded from her assessable income. The portion of the capital gain that's liable to tax is calculated as follows:

Capital proceeds (sale price)		$750000
Less:		
Cost base:		
First element:		
Purchase price	$350000	
Second element:		
Stamp duty (buying)	$12000	
Legal fees (buying)	$1000	
Agent's commission (selling)	$18000	
Advertising costs (selling)	$2000	

Legal fees (selling)	$1 000	
Fourth element:		
Capital improvements	$50 000	$434 000
Notional capital gain		$316 000
Less:		
50% CGT discount		$158 000
Capital gain		$158 000

As Hannah owned her rental property for more than 12 months and makes a $316 000 capital gain on the sale, only half the capital gain ($158 000) is taxable. The other half is exempt from tax. Note: in this case the third element of the cost base is ignored because these costs were previously claimed as tax-deductible expenses.

 Tax tip

Under the CGT concessions for small business, if you operate a small business and you make a capital gain on the sale of active assets (such as your business premises or factory), the capital gain can be reduced to nil. These concessions are available to sole traders, partners in a partnership, companies and trusts (see chapter 8). However, they're not available if your business entity owns an investment property that derives passive income such as rent. Incidentally, under the Tax Act you're considered to be carrying on a small business if your annual turnover (sales) is less than $2 million. For a comprehensive discussion on all the conditions you'll need to satisfy, the Tax Office has issued a publication titled

Am I eligible for the small business entity concessions? You can download a copy from its website <www.ato.gov.au>. See also appendix A, Active asset (deriving rent).

 Tax trap

If you have bought an income-producing property after 13 May 1997 and qualify for capital-works deductions, you will need to deduct them from the cost base to calculate the amount of the capital gain that's liable to tax. For more details see chapter 3.

Property bought between 20 September 1985 and 21 September 1999

There are two ways to calculate a capital gain if you sell a property that you bought between 20 September 1985 and 21 September 1999. They are referred to as the 'discount method' and the 'indexation method'. The Tax Act allows you to choose the method that will result in you paying the least amount of tax. Fortunately this is not going to be a difficult decision to make. As many years have now passed since these new rules were introduced in 1999, you will find the discount method to be the better option, as illustrated in the following case studies that compare the discount method and indexation method.

Using the discount method

The discount method follows the same rules you use to calculate a 'discount capital gain'. As you have owned the property for more than 12 months, only 50 per cent of the capital gain you make on disposal is taxable. The other 50 per cent is exempt and excluded from your assessable income.

Incidentally, if you want to quickly work out in your head how much tax you're up for if you a sell a property you've owned for more than 12 months, the ball park answer is around a quarter of the capital gain you make on the sale (ouch!).

Case study: using the discount method

On 23 March 1990 Travis paid $125 000 for a rental property. The incidental costs associated with the purchase were $6000 for stamp duty and $500 for legal fees. Travis sells the property today for $800 000. The incidental costs associated with selling the property are $19 500 for the agent's commission, $2000 for advertising costs and $1000 for legal fees. As Travis purchased the property before 21 September 1999, he has the option to use either the 'discount method' or the 'indexation method' to calculate the amount of capital gain that's liable to tax.

If Travis uses the discount method only 50 per cent of the capital gain is taxable. The balance of course is exempt. Under this method the portion of the capital gain that's taxable is calculated as follows:

Capital proceeds (sale price)		$800 000
Less:		
Cost base:		
First element:		
Purchase price	$125 000	
Second element:		
Stamp duty (buying)	$6 000	
Legal fees (buying)	$500	
Agent's commission (selling)	$19 500	
Advertising (selling)	$2 000	
Legal fees (selling)	$1 000	$154 000
Notional capital gain		$646 000
Less		
50% CGT discount		$323 000
Capital gain		$323 000

If Travis elects to use the discount method he's only liable to pay tax on half the capital gain he made on disposal (namely $323 000). The other half is exempt from tax and excluded from assessable income.

Case study: using the indexation method

Under the 'indexation method' (which was the way you calculated a capital gain before 21 September 1999), you can adjust the purchase price and incidental costs of purchase for inflation. The consumer price index is used to make this adjustment (see table 4.1 on p. 89). A major limitation with this method is that you can only adjust for inflation for the period between the date you bought the property and 30 September 1999. As many years have passed since the new rules were introduced, this method is of academic interest only. Nevertheless, I always say it doesn't do any harm to do the calculation to check how much tax you're going to save using the discount method.

So if Travis were to use the indexation method he'll need to adjust the purchase price ($125000) and incidental costs of purchase ($6500 for stamp duty and legal fees) for inflation for the period between the date he bought the property (23 March 1990) and 30 September 1999. The following formula is used to make the relevant adjustment and the necessary cost price index figures you'll need to use are taken from table 4.1.

CPI at 30 September 1999 $\dfrac{(123.4)}{(100.9)} = 1.222$
CPI at date of purchase

As Travis had purchased the rental property and incurred all his incidental costs of purchase in the CPI quarter ending 31 March 1990, the CPI figure to do the above calculation is 100.9. Note: under this method any additional costs you incur after 21 September 1999 cannot be adjusted for inflation as they were incurred after 1999. If Travis elects to use the indexation method, the portion of the capital gain that's taxable is calculated as follows:

Capital proceeds (sale price)	$800000
Less:	
Indexation cost base:	
First element:	
Purchase price	$152750
($125000 × 1.222)	
Second element:	
Stamp duty ($6000 × 1.222)	$7332

Legal fees ($500 × 1.222)	$611	
Agent's commission (selling)	$19 500	
Advertising (selling)	$2 000	
Legal fees (selling)	$1 000	$183 193
Capital gain		$616 807

Under the indexation method the amount of the capital gain that's taxable is $616 807. It goes without saying it would be more beneficial for Travis to choose the discount method as only $323 000 is taxable.

Table 4.1: consumer price index

Year	31 March	30 June	30 September	31 December
1985	0	0	71.3	72.7
1986	74.4	75.6	77.6	79.8
1987	81.4	82.6	84.0	85.5
1988	87.0	88.5	90.2	92.0
1989	92.9	95.2	97.4	99.2
1990	**100.9**	102.5	103.3	106.0
1991	105.8	106.0	106.6	107.6
1992	107.6	107.3	107.4	107.9
1993	108.9	109.3	109.8	110.0
1994	110.4	111.2	111.9	112.8
1995	114.7	116.2	117.6	118.5
1996	119.0	119.8	120.1	120.3
1997	120.5	120.2	119.7	120.0
1998	120.3	121.0	121.3	121.9
1999	121.8	122.3	**123.4**	

Source: Australian Bureau of Statistics.

Tax trap

Under Australian tax law if you merely realise a capital asset to its best advantage (for instance, you subdivide a large block of land you have owned for many years into smaller blocks to enhance the sale price—see appendix A, Business Activity (or mere realisation of a capital asset)—the transaction is likely to fall for consideration under the CGT provisions. This means you could qualify for a 50 per cent CGT discount if you have owned the property for more than 12 months. But if your activities go beyond merely realising a capital asset (for instance, you also decide to put in roads and sewage, and construct buildings), the Tax Office may consider you to be carrying on a property business, in which case the entire profit you make on the sale is taxable. As this can be a complicated part of tax law, it's best that you seek professional advice if you're considering doing the above. For more details see appendix A, Business activity (or mere realisation of asset), and particularly the various tax cases relating to this issue.

Capital loss

Under the CGT provisions your capacity to claim a capital loss is somewhat limited, as you can't deduct it from other assessable income you may derive such as your salary and wages, business profits and investment income. This is because a capital loss can only be deducted from a capital gain. So if you make no capital gains in the financial year that you incur a capital loss, the capital loss can be carried forward for an indefinite period, and deducted from capital gains you make in the future. You'll need to keep an accurate record of any capital losses you make that can be deducted from future capital gains. Incidentally, if you incur a capital loss on a property transaction, you can deduct it from a capital gain you may make on the sale of another category of CGT assets, such as shares.

 Tax trap

In the event of your death, if you have any capital losses not yet recouped they can't be transferred to your beneficiaries. This is because capital losses can only be utilised during your lifetime.

Case study: calculating a capital loss

Eight years ago Kevin purchased a block of land. The purchase price was $300000. The incidental costs associated with the purchase were $7000 in stamp duty and $1000 in legal fees. Kevin sells his block of land today. The sale price is $280000. The incidental costs he incurs in the sale are $5000 for the agent's commission and $1000 in legal fees.

Capital proceeds (sale price) $280000
Less:
Reduced cost base:
First element:

Purchase price (buying)	$300 000	
Second element:		
Stamp duty (buying)	$7 000	
Legal fees (buying)	$1 000	
Agent's commission (selling)	$5 000	
Legal fees (selling)	$1 000	$314 000
Capital loss		$34 000

Note: when calculating a capital loss the third element of the cost base (non-deductible holding costs) cannot be taken into account, as they can't be used to create or increase a capital loss (see Non-deductible holding costs).

In this case Kevin makes a $34 000 capital loss. This capital loss can only be deducted from a capital gain. If Kevin makes no capital gains in the same financial year that he incurs the capital loss, the capital loss can be offset against any capital gains Kevin makes in future years. Note: when calculating a capital loss you'll need to use the reduced cost base. The reduced cost base is similar to the cost base of a CGT asset minus certain expenditure that has previously been allowed as a tax deduction (such as capital works deductions—see chapter 3).

 Tax trap

If you incur a capital loss on the sale of a CGT asset (such as real estate) that you acquired before 21 September 1999, you cannot index the cost base for inflation (as is the case if you make a capital gain).

Non-deductible holding costs

Under Australian tax law, if you have bought a non-income-producing property since 20 August 1991 that you intend to use for your personal use and enjoyment (for instance, a holiday home or block of land), non-deductible holding costs such as interest on borrowings to buy the property, council rates and land taxes, insurance and repairs are not tax deductible. This is because the property is not used to derive assessable income.

But all is not lost! Under the CGT provisions these costs can be added to the property's cost base, and can be taken into account if you make a capital gain on the sale (see How a capital gain is calculated on p. 77, and more particularly the third element of the cost base). Unfortunately, non-deductible holding costs cannot be taken into account to create or increase a capital loss. Further, for property purchased before 30 September 1999, any non-deductible costs you incurred cannot be adjusted for inflation. You will need to keep an accurate record of all the non-deductible holding costs you incur over the years.

Case study: non-deductible holding costs

Eight years ago Anita purchased a holiday home at a popular holiday resort for her personal use and enjoyment. The purchase price was $250 000. The incidental costs associated with the purchase were $6000 for stamp duty and $1000 in legal fees. Anita sells the property today. The sale price is $500 000. The incidental costs relating to the sale of the property are $12 000 for the agent's commission and $1000 in legal fees. During the period of time Anita owned the property, her non-deductible holding costs (such as interest on borrowings, council rates and land taxes, insurance and repairs) amounted to $50 000. As her holiday home was purchased after 20 August 1991 Anita can add her non-deductible holding costs to the property's cost base. These costs can only be taken into account if Anita makes a capital gain, but they cannot be used to create or increase a capital loss.

Capital proceeds (sale price)		$500 000
Less:		
Cost base:		
First element:		
Purchase price	$250 000	
Second element:		
Stamp duty (buying)	$6 000	
Legal fees (buying)	$1 000	
Agent's commission (selling)	$12 000	
Legal fees (selling)	$1 000	
Third element:		
Non-deductible holding costs	$50 000	$320 000
Notional capital gain		$180 000
Less:		
50% CGT discount		$90 000
Capital gain		$90 000

As Anita owned the property for more than 12 months only $90 000 of the capital gain is taxable. The balance is exempt. On the other hand, if the sale price was $260 000 (rather than $500 000), Anita would have made a $10 000 capital loss ($260 000 – $270 000 = –$10 000). Under these circumstances, Anita cannot take the $50 000 non-deductible holding costs into account because these costs cannot be used to create or increase a capital loss.

 Tax trap

If you permanently leave Australia you will be deemed to have disposed of your CGT assets (such as real estate) at their market value. However, you can avoid paying any CGT if you elect the CGT assets you own (for instance, your property holdings) to be 'taxable Australian property'. If you do this no tax is payable until they're eventually sold, or if unsold, until you decide to become an Australian resident again.

Property from a deceased estate

The CGT treatment of property from a deceased estate depends on when the deceased originally acquired it or whether it was their main residence. Under the CGT provisions the following rules apply.

- Death is not a CGT event, which means no potential CGT liability arises when someone dies.

- If the deceased acquired a property before 20 September 1985, the beneficiary is deemed to have acquired the property on the date of death at its market value.

- If the deceased acquired a property on or after 20 September 1985, the beneficiary is deemed to have acquired the property on the date of death at the value the deceased originally acquired it (namely the deceased's cost base). This means the beneficiary is liable to pay CGT on any increase in value during the time the deceased owned the property, plus any further increase in value during the time the beneficiary owns it.

- The deceased's main residence will continue to be exempt under the CGT provisions, provided the beneficiary treats the property as their main residence. Alternatively, if the property is sold within two years of the deceased's death no CGT is payable. This will be the case even if the property was leased during this period of time (see chapter 5).

Case study: inheriting a pre–20 September 1985 property

Margaret purchased a rental property in 1984. The cost price was $100 000. Margaret dies in 2011 and bequeaths the property to her son Geoffrey. The property's market value on the date of death is $600 000. Geoffrey is treated as having acquired the property on the date of death at its market value

($600000). This will become the cost base under the CGT provisions. Geoffrey then sells the property one year later for $650000 and makes a $50000 capital gain ($650000 − $600000 = $50000). As the property was owned overall for more than 12 months, only 50 per cent of the capital gain is taxable. Conversely, if Geoffrey sells the property for $550000 he will make a $50000 capital loss.

Case study: inheriting a post–20 September 1985 property

Mark purchased a rental property in 2001. The cost price was $250000. Mark dies in 2011 and bequeaths the property to his daughter Emma. The property's market value on the date of death is $600000. As the deceased acquired the property after 20 September 1985 the property is a post-CGT asset. Under these circumstances, Emma is treated as having acquired the property on the date of death at the value that Mark originally paid for it ($250000). In this case the property's market value ($600000) has no relevance as the property is a post-CGT asset. Emma sells the property one year later for $650000 and makes a $400000 capital gain ($650000 − $250000 = $400000). But there is some relief. As the property had been owned overall for more than 12 months, Emma can claim a 50 per cent CGT discount which means only $200000 is taxable.

Tax tip

For a comprehensive discussion on the meaning of 'market value' see the Tax Office publication *Market valuation for tax purposes* and more particularly the section 'What "market value" means'. See also appendix A, Market value (meaning).

Useful references

Australian Taxation Office publications

- *Guide to capital gains tax (NAT 4152)*
- *Capital gains tax checklist*

Australian Taxation Office interpretative decisions

- ID 2002/633: *Income tax: capital gains tax: demolition of a dwelling: CGT event C1*

- ID 2003/635: *Income tax: CGT: capital proceeds payable by instalments — not all received — no reduction of capital proceeds received*

- ID 2003/938: *Income tax: assessability of capital gain derived by non-resident from sale of real property situated in Australia*

CHAPTER 5

This is where I reside and it's all tax free

There's an unwritten law deeply embedded in Australian folklore that states the great Australian dream is to own your own home, or as the Tax Office calls it, your 'main residence'. Owning a main residence is a great feeling you may like to experience. But wait, there's more! Under Australian tax law your main residence is exempt under the capital gains tax provisions (see chapter 4). From a tax planning point of view this could prove a shrewd investment if your property increases substantially in value. But as they say in the classics, conditions apply. To gain this significant tax benefit you can't use your main residence to derive assessable income (for instance, by carrying on a business from home). If this is the case you'll only qualify for a partial exemption. In this chapter I discuss the tax issues relating to owning a main residence.

Meaning of main residence

Under Australian tax law a main residence is a place where you and your family normally reside and use primarily for private or domestic purposes (such as a house, flat, unit or townhouse). Technically speaking, the Income Tax Assessment Act defines a main residence as a unit of accommodation that:

- is a building or is contained in a building and consists wholly or mainly of residential accommodation

- is a caravan, houseboat, or other mobile home.

It also includes any land immediately under the unit of accommodation and up to two hectares of land surrounding your property, plus any structures normally associated with owning a home such as a garage and storeroom.

At a glance: main residence — the rules you need to know

- Your main residence is ordinarily exempt from CGT.

- Your main residence can include up to two hectares of land on which your dwelling is built.

- You can only own one main residence.

- A main residence can include a detached granny flat built in the backyard, a structure built underground (for instance, you live in Coober Pedy) and a yacht. But a tent does not usually satisfy the condition for a main-residence exemption (which is no big deal if you don't like living in a tent!).

- To qualify for a main-residence exemption you must ordinarily reside in the property for at least three months; see appendix A, Main-residence exemption.

- Intention to reside in a property is not sufficient to qualify for a main-residence exemption; see appendix A, Main-residence exemption.

 Tax tip

If the land surrounding your main residence exceeds the two hectares limit, you can calculate the cost base of the land on a pro-rata area basis when determining the portion of the land that will be exempt from tax. You can also nominate the best two hectares as being part of your main residence!

 Tax trap

If your company owns a residential property that you use as your main residence, the company cannot claim a main-residence exemption. This is because only individuals can own a main residence. To make matters worse a company cannot claim a 50 per cent CGT discount if it sells the property 12 months after buying it and makes a capital gain on sale (see chapters 4 and 8).

Main residence: financing the purchase

Depending on where you live, the price of a residential property can vary upwards from $200 000 to well over a few million dollars. According to a recent international report on housing affordability, Australian house prices are among the most expensive in the English-speaking world! Raising the necessary finance and endeavouring to repay the principal plus interest at regular intervals could prove a difficult exercise to manage (especially if you have a large family to support as well).

In addition to paying the purchase price, you may also be liable to pay a 10 per cent goods and services tax (GST). This is normally the case if you buy a new residential property or a property that has been substantially renovated (see chapter 3). Not only that, but you may also be liable to pay certain incidental costs such as the stamp duty that Australian state and territory governments levy on property transactions, legal fees and loan establishment fees. To add salt to the home purchasing wound, as your main residence is not used to derive assessable income (for instance, rent), you cannot claim expenditure such as interest on borrowings, council rates, insurance and repairs as a tax-deductible expense.

The only consolation is that your main residence is exempt from tax, which is nice to have up your sleeve if the capital gain is likely to be substantial (see Main-residence exemption on p. 108).

Figure 5.1: first home buyer concessions

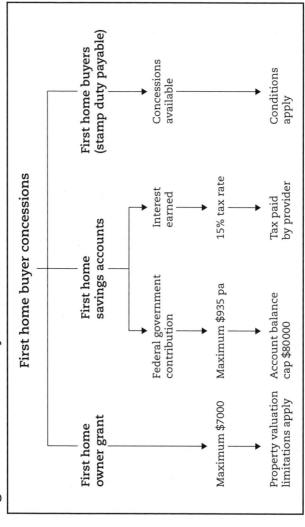

Getting some financial relief

The federal, state and territory governments of Australia have introduced a number of schemes to help you raise the necessary funds to buy or build your main residence (see figure 5.1). But there are certain conditions you'll need to satisfy before you can access them. The three main-residence concessions available to first home buyers are listed here.

First home owner grant

To help you cover any additional costs you're likely to incur when buying or building a dwelling, you could qualify for a $7000 first home owner grant. This grant is administered by the various state and territory governments of Australia, and is only available to buy or build a residential property that does not exceed a certain price valuation (see table 5.1). Incidentally, this scheme is only available to residents of Australia and the grant is not liable to income tax. One major condition is that you and your partner must not have previously owned a property, and you'll need to reside in your main residence for at least six months. For more information you can visit your state or territory government website (see table 5.2).

Table 5.1: first home owner grant

Jurisdiction	Limits on property valuations
ACT	No limit at time of writing
NSW	$750000
NT	$750000

Jurisdiction	Limits on property valuations
Qld	$750 000
SA	No limit at time of writing
Tas.	No limit at time of writing
Vic.	$750 000
WA	$750 000 (north of 26th parallel, $1 000 000)

Table 5.2: state and territory government revenue offices

Jurisdiction	State and territory government websites
ACT	<www.revenue.act.gov.au>
NSW	<www.osr.nsw.gov.au>
NT	<www.nt.gov.au>
Qld	<www.osr.qld.gov.au>
SA	<ww.revenuesa.sa.gov.au>
Tas.	<www.treasury.tas.gov.au>
Vic.	<www.sro.vic.gov.au>
WA	<www.dtf.wa.gov.au>

 Tax trap

The Tax Office has issued a ruling stating that if you receive a first home owner grant, you'll need to exclude from the cost base of the property expenditure an amount equal to the grant you receive. This is because the grant is considered to be a recoupment of that expenditure. This is relevant

> **Tax trap** *(cont'd)*
>
> if you're only entitled to a partial main-residence exemption (for instance because you used part of your home to produce assessable income).

First home saver account

In 2008 the federal government introduced a scheme to help you save for a deposit to buy or build your first home. Under this scheme if you make an after-tax contribution into a first home saver account, the federal government will make a 17 per cent contribution on your behalf. This means if you contribute the maximum permitted each year (currently $5500), the federal government will put in $935 ($5500 × 17% = $935). The scheme also allows you to make further (non-qualifying) contributions into this account each financial year. But there is a cap (or limit) on how much you can have in this account. The account balance cap is currently $80 000, after which you can no longer make a personal contribution. Incidentally, the various amounts mentioned above are indexed periodically in $500 increments. In the meantime, any interest the account earns is taxed at the rate of 15 per cent (and this tax is paid by the account provider!). When you decide to withdraw the funds to buy or build your first home the withdrawals are tax-free. One major condition is that you'll need to live in the property for at least six months within the first 12 months of the purchase or construction. This benefit is in addition to the $7000 first home owner grant that's available to first home owners! For more details you can read the Tax Office publication *First home saver accounts—common questions*. You can download a copy from the Tax Office website <www.ato.gov.au>.

Stamp duty relief

When you purchase a property you're ordinarily liable to pay stamp duty, which is imposed by the state and territory governments of Australia. Stamp duty is levied on a progressive basis. So the higher the purchase price the more stamp duty you're liable to pay. The amount you actually pay depends on the state or territory in which you reside. With respect to first home buyers you may be eligible for concessions or exemptions if you satisfy certain conditions (see table 5.3). For more information you can visit your state or territory government website (see table 5.2 on p. 105).

Table 5.3: stamp duty: first home buyer

Jurisdiction	$500 000 primary residence, effective 2010–11 financial year
ACT	$20 500
NSW	$0
NT	$5913
Qld	$0
SA	$21 330
Tas.	$17 550
Vic.	$21 970
WA	$0

Tax tip

If you're planning to borrow money to buy your main residence, it's generally accepted that your interest and principal repayments should not exceed 30 per cent of your household income, and the purchase price should not exceed four times your household income. Household income is gross income before tax that you and/or your partner normally derive from various sources. For instance, if your household income is $150 000 per annum, according to this rule of thumb, the purchase price should not exceed $600 000 ($150 000 × 4 = $600 000), and your mortgage repayments should not exceed $45 000 per annum ($150 000 × 30% = $45 000). From a tax planning point of view, as your interest repayments are not tax deductible, it's best that you pay off the mortgage as quickly as possible.

Main-residence exemption

Under the CGT provisions your main residence is ordinarily exempt from CGT. From a tax planning point of view this could prove to be a great way of building wealth that will not be liable to tax. As properties in good locations tend to double in value every seven to ten years, you'll be in a position to keep the entire proceeds of sale (less incidental costs to sell it).

To gain this major concession the property must be used primarily for private or domestic purposes, and you can't use it to derive assessable income. For example, if you carry on a business (for instance an accounting practice or doctor's surgery) from your main residence, only part of your main residence is exempt from tax. The portions that will be exempt and non-exempt are normally determined on an area basis. For example, your home consists of 12 equal sized rooms and you use three rooms to derive assessable income. Under these circumstances, one quarter of your main residence is liable to CGT and three quarters will be exempt from CGT.

 Tax tip

If you buy a property adjacent to your main residence (for instance, your next-door neighbour's block of land), you can include it as part of your main residence. This is on the condition that you don't exceed the two hectares limit rule and you use it primarily for private or domestic purposes. There is a further condition that if you sell your main residence at a later date, you'll need to sell both holdings simultaneously to the new owner in order to qualify for a full CGT exemption.

 Tax trap

If you subdivide your main residence and sell off part of the surplus land, the part you sell off is liable to CGT. This is because a main-residence exemption

Tax trap *(cont'd)*

only applies if you sell your property in its entirety. If you do subdivide, you'll need to apportion the property's cost base at the time of subdivision, to work out whether you have made a capital gain or capital loss on disposal.

You can only own one main residence

Under the CGT provisions you can only own one main residence for the purposes of qualifying for a CGT exemption. If your spouse or partner also happens to own a main residence, you'll need to nominate one property for which you intend to claim the main-residence exemption. From a tax planning point of view, it's best to nominate the property that's more likely to give you the bigger capital gain if you subsequently sell it, as no CGT is payable! Alternatively, if you can't decide, you can elect to use 50 per cent of each of the properties you own as your main residence.

 Tax tip

If you buy a new main residence while you're still in the process of selling your existing main residence, both properties will ordinarily be exempt from CGT for a period of up to six months.

Home office expenses

If you are an employee or you carry on a business you may be required to do some work at home rather than at your regular place of employment; for example, you're a school teacher and it's more convenient to mark your student assignments at home. Under these circumstances, you may be entitled to claim certain 'running expenses' in respect to maintaining a home office. Under Australian tax law, the types of running expenses you can claim are generally confined to expenditure such as:

- cleaning of your home office

- depreciation of your computer

- depreciation of office furniture (such as a desk, chairs, bookcase and cabinet)

- heating/cooling and lighting

- repairing your office furniture and equipment

- telephone calls.

You'll need to keep receipts and record the method you use to claim a portion of these expenses as a tax deduction. The Tax Office has advised that you can claim your home-office expenses based on the actual expenses you incur, or you can use a fixed hourly rate of 26 cents per hour, which means you'll need to keep a record of the number of hours you use your home office. The Tax Office has issued a 'Home office expenses calculator' to help you work out how much you can claim each year.

You can find this tax tool calculator on the Tax Office website <www.ato.gov.au>.

Unless you work from home and your home office is your place of business, you can't claim a tax deduction for 'occupancy expenses' such as rent, interest on a mortgage, council rates, insurance and repairs. The Tax Office has ruled that these expenses are private or domestic in nature and not tax deductible. Unfortunately, if you do qualify for a tax deduction, under the CGT provisions, your main residence will no longer be fully exempt from tax if you sell the property at a later date (see Main-residence exemption on p. 108). From a tax planning point of view, if you live in a place where property values are skyrocketing, it may be best to work from rented premises to preserve your main-residence exemption status. Keep in mind the rent you pay is ordinarily a tax deductible expense.

 Tax tip

If you lease a property that was your former main residence, under the CGT provisions, you will be treated as having acquired the property after it ceases to be your main residence for its market value.

Temporary absence rule

If you're absent from your main residence (for instance, you're posted overseas or interstate), under the 'temporary absence rule' your property can continue to be treated as your main residence while you're away. In the meantime, if you buy another property, you can't treat that one as your main residence as well (as you cannot own two main residences). This is also the case if, for example, your spouse and one of your children live in one location (say, Melbourne) and you and another child live in another location (say, Sydney).

If you do not lease your dwelling while you're absent, your property can be treated as your main residence for an indefinite period. On the other hand, if you lease your main residence while you're away, your property will continue to be exempt from CGT for a maximum period of six years. To add icing to the main-residence exemption cake, expenditure such as interest on a mortgage, council rates, insurance and repairs you incur will now be tax deductible! If you want the exemption period to continue beyond the six-year limit, you'll need to reoccupy the property again. If you do this and leave at a later date (for instance, after six months), you can again lease your main residence for a further maximum period of six years!

Property bought before 20 September 1985

If you currently reside in a property that you purchased before 20 September 1985, the property is excluded from the CGT provisions (see chapter 4). If you decide to buy another property and treat that one as your main residence you will now own two properties that are exempt from CGT. Incidentally, the fact that your pre-CGT property happens to be your main residence is irrelevant as the property is specifically excluded from the CGT provisions. If you decide to move back to your pre-CGT property at a later date, under the temporary absence rule, you can lease the property you treated as your new main residence for a period not exceeding six years, without affecting its exemption status. Alternatively, if you do not lease it (for instance, you use it primarily for private or domestic purposes), the property will continue to be exempt from CGT for an indefinite period (see Temporary absence rule on p. 112).

 Tax trap

If you sell your main residence and make a capital loss, the capital loss cannot be deducted from a capital gain you make on disposal of another CGT asset. This is because your main residence is exempt under the CGT provisions.

Case study: how to have your cake and eat it too!

John and Betty, who are both 61 years of age, reside in a much sought-after city location where property values have increased substantially in recent years. Their main residence was purchased in 1998. They want to retire immediately but only have a combined amount of $200 000 in their complying superannuation funds. They are also eager to buy a

$200 000 property that's up for sale in a little fishing village in southern New South Wales, where they would like to spend their time in retirement. From a tax planning point of view John and Betty could consider the following option.

⇒ Withdraw the $200 000 from their super funds and purchase the property in southern New South Wales. If they do this they will own and reside in a property that has the potential to increase in value. As they are both over 60 years of age, the $200 000 they withdraw from their respective funds is exempt from tax (see chapter 8).

⇒ Nominate their 1998 city property as their main residence, even while they're absent and living in their fishing village property.

⇒ While they're absent they can lease their 1998 city property to help supplement their income in retirement. To add icing to the retirement cake, under the CGT temporary absence rule their 1998 city property can continue to be treated as their main residence for up to six years while they're away. If they do this over the next six years they will derive rent from leasing their 1998 city property plus *the potential to derive further capital growth* that's not liable to tax!

⇒ If they decide to sell their 1998 city property at the end of six years, the entire capital gain they make on sale is exempt from CGT. Alternatively, if they want the 1998 city property to continue to be exempt from tax, they'll need to return to their existing main residence. They could reoccupy their fishing village property at a later date, and lease their existing main residence again for a further six years (which will continue to be exempt from tax under the CGT temporary absence rule!).

 Tax tip

The following CGT rules apply if you inherit someone's main residence (for instance, from your parents). If you decide to keep the property and treat it as your main residence, the property will continue to be exempt from CGT. From a tax planning point of view, this may be worth contemplating if the property is in a good location and property valuations are skyrocketing. Alternatively, if you sell it, no CGT is payable if the property is sold within two years of the deceased's date of death. This is the case even if you were to lease the property during these two years.

Useful references

Australian Taxation Office publications

- *First home saver accounts — what qualifies as owning a home? (NAT 72453)*

- *Is the dwelling your main residence?*

Australian Taxation Office interpretative decisions

- ID 2003/109: *Capital gains tax: capital gains tax: Deceased estate — main residence exemption*

- ID 2003/232: *Income tax: capital gains tax: main residence exemption — demolition and reconstruction of dwelling*

- ID 2003/785: *Income tax: capital gains tax: main residence exemption — spouse choosing a dwelling as main residence*

Other taxation rulings

- TD 92/158: *Income tax: capital gains: can the following comprise a 'dwelling' and therefore be eligible for exemption as a sole or principal residence (i) a structure built underground? (ii) a yacht? (iii) a tent?*

- TR 93/30: *Income tax: deductions for home office expenses*

- TD 1999/69: *Income tax: capital gains: can the term 'dwelling' as defined in section 118-115 of the Income Tax Assessment Act 1997 include more than one unit of accommodation?*

Chapter 6

Investing in an overseas property: going global

Buying an overseas property gives you the opportunity to own a dwelling in a particular overseas location (for instance, at a popular holiday resort), where you can reside when you retire or stay while you're on holidays. To add icing to the foreign investment cake, you can derive rent if you lease the property plus there is opportunity for capital growth if your property increases in value. With the Australian dollar appreciating in recent years; this could prove a shrewd investment opportunity to consider, especially if property prices are much cheaper overseas. You may also find certain countries (for instance, New Zealand) do not charge stamp duty on property purchases or a capital gains tax if you make a profit on sale. In this chapter I discuss how you're taxed if you own a property outside Australia.

Foreign rent

Under Australian tax law residents of Australia are liable to pay tax on assessable income they derive from worldwide sources during the year of income. This will be the case even if you're liable to pay foreign tax on assessable income you derive overseas (such as rent from an overseas rental property). If you're liable to pay foreign tax you may be entitled to claim a foreign income tax offset for the amount of foreign tax you paid. Incidentally, all foreign income you derive and foreign deductible expenses you incur, and any foreign tax you pay, must be converted into Australian dollars. For more details see the Tax Office publication *Converting foreign income to Australian dollars*.

Any foreign-source rent you receive must be disclosed in your Australian income tax return at 'Item 20: Foreign-source income and foreign assets or property', located in your tax return for individuals (supplementary section). You must also disclose at Item 20 any foreign income tax offset you are entitled to claim.

 Tax trap

If you're planning to buy an overseas rental property it's best that you do your homework to familiarise yourself with the local tax rules before you sign on the dotted line. You should check out whether you're liable to pay tax at the time you buy an overseas property (such as stamp duty that's levied on a property purchased in Australia), how rent is assessed, what types of tax deductions you can claim, how much income tax you're liable to pay, and how you're taxed if you make a capital gain on sale. This is to avoid any nasty surprises that may not appeal to you. I always say it's better to be safe than sorry!

Case study: claiming a foreign income tax offset

Barbara owns a rental property in England. According to her accounting records, at the end of the financial year she had received $12 000 rent and pays United Kingdom (UK) tax amounting to $3000. Barbara needs to include the $12 000 rent as part of her Australian assessable income, and is liable to pay Australian income tax on this amount as well. She can also claim any losses and outgoings she incurs in deriving her UK rental income in her Australian tax return. However, Australia has entered into double tax agreement provisions with certain countries (such as the UK). So, as Barbara is paying tax in the UK, under these provisions she can claim a $3000 foreign income tax offset. Barbara needs to have documentary evidence (for instance, a notice of assessment or receipt) to substantiate the fact that she has *paid* UK tax amounting to $3000.

At a glance: how you're taxed

This is how you're taxed if you own an overseas rental property:

- Foreign rent you derive is liable to Australian income tax.

- Foreign expenses you incur in deriving foreign rent may qualify as a tax-deductible expense.

- Net foreign rental losses you incur can be deducted from other Australian-sourced assessable income you derive.

- A capital gain on disposal of an overseas property is liable to Australian income tax, but only half the gain is assessable if the property is held for more than 12 months.

- Capital losses can be offset against other capital gains you derive.

- You may be entitled to claim a foreign income tax offset in respect of any foreign tax you paid.

Claiming a tax deduction

The good news here is that if you invest in an overseas rental property you can claim the same types of deductions that you can for domestic rental properties. This means you can claim expenses you incur in deriving your overseas rental income, such as:

- capital works deductions

- depreciation

- interest on borrowings to purchase your overseas rental property

- rates, insurance and repairs

- real estate agents' fees to collect the rent

- travel costs to inspect your overseas property (see the Tax Office publication *Rental properties—claiming travel expenses deductions* to qualify for this deduction).

If your foreign rental expenses were to exceed your foreign rental income, the net loss you incur can be deducted from any other Australian-sourced assessable income you derive (such as salary and wages, business profits and investment income).

 Tax tip

If you own an overseas property you'll need to keep accurate records of:

⇒ the purchase price (contract of purchase)

⇒ any gross rent you derive overseas (rental statements)

⇒ any deductible expenses you incur in deriving your rental income (such as invoices and receipts)

⇒ any foreign tax you pay for the foreign income you derived (for instance, a notice of assessment).

Tax tip *(cont'd)*

If you travel overseas to inspect your rental property you must justify the reason for your visit and keep a record of your accommodation and travel costs (invoices).

Capital gains tax and overseas properties

Under the capital gains tax (CGT) provisions, you're liable to pay CGT if you sell a CGT asset you acquire on or after 20 September 1985 and you make a capital gain (see chapter 4). This is the case if you sell an overseas investment property or holiday home that you keep for your personal use and enjoyment while overseas. Any foreign capital gains (or losses) you make on disposal must be disclosed in your Australian tax return.

If you have owned the property for more than 12 months, only 50 per cent of the capital gain you make on disposal is liable to tax. On the other hand, if you make a capital loss, the capital loss can only be deducted from a capital gain you make on disposal of other CGT assets that you own (see chapter 4). As is the case with foreign rental income, if you're liable to pay foreign tax on any capital gain you make on disposal of your overseas property, you may be entitled to claim a foreign income tax offset for the amount you paid.

Tax tip

If you are a non-resident and you become a resident of Australia; certain CGT assets that you own overseas (for instance, real estate you purchased after 19 September 1985), will fall for consideration under the CGT provisions. You'll be treated as having acquired your CGT assets at their market value at the time you become a resident. For more details see the Tax Office publication *Capital gains in Australia*, particularly the section 'Becoming a resident'.

Tax trap

If you are a non-resident and you own a rental property in Australia you will need to lodge an Australian tax return and pay tax on the amount of rent you receive during the financial year. This is because non-residents are liable to pay tax on income sourced in Australia.

Useful references

Australian Taxation Office publications

- *Converting foreign income to Australian dollars*
- *Guide to foreign income tax offset rules (NAT 72923)*

- *Investing in overseas property*

- *Investing overseas — overview*

- *Personal investors guide to capital gains tax (NAT 4152)*

- *Tax-smart investing: what Australians investing in overseas property need to know*

- *Reporting foreign income*

Australian Taxation Office interpretative decisions

- ID 2002/71: *Income tax: assessability of rental income received from New Zealand — foreign tax credits*

- ID 2003/1079: *Income tax: assessability of rental income received from real property situated in the People's Republic of China*

- ID 2005/207: *Income tax: assessability of rental income received from real property situated in the United Kingdom (UK) by a dual resident of Australia and the UK*

- ID 2006/71: *Income tax: assessability of capital gain on sale of a property from the Netherlands*

- ID 2009/93: *Income tax: assessability of rental income received by Australian resident from the United Kingdom*

CHAPTER 7

Bankrolling your property purchases: money makes money

A major snag with investing in real estate is that you need to have a substantial amount of money to buy a property outright. With the median price of a residential property in Australia at around $500 000, you may need to borrow the necessary funds to help bankroll your property purchases. Under Australian tax law, if you borrow money to buy an income-producing property, such as a rental property, the interest and borrowing costs you incur are ordinarily tax-deductible expenses. In this chapter, I discuss the key tax issues you'll need to consider to comply with the Income Tax Assessment Act.

Payment of interest: the purpose or use test

Under Australian tax law, deductibility of interest is determined by examining the purpose or use of the loan; see appendix A, Borrowing funds (purpose or use test). If the purpose of the loan is to buy a rental property the interest payments are tax-deductible expenses. This is also the case if the purpose of the loan is to construct a rental property.

On the other hand, if the loan is partly used for the purpose of deriving assessable income, you can only claim a tax deduction to the extent that it is used to derive assessable income. For example, if you buy a shop that you intend to lease (or carry on a business in), and you plan to reside at the back of the premises, you can only claim interest for the part of the loan that relates to the shop. The balance is not deductible. But if the purpose of the loan is to buy a non-income-producing property (for instance, a holiday home or block of land) the interest is not tax deductible. This is because the property is used for private or domestic purposes and not to derive assessable income. However, the good news here is that under the capital gains tax (CGT) provisions, the non-deductible interest can be added to the property's cost base, and can be taken into account if you sell the property and make a capital gain (see chapter 4).

Tax trap

If you borrow money to buy a rental property, the interest is ordinarily a tax-deductible expense. But if you change your mind at a later date and use the property for a private or domestic purpose, the interest will no longer be tax deductible.

At a glance: incorrectly claiming an interest deduction

The Tax Office has identified the following common mistakes when claiming interest as a tax-deductible expense:

- claiming interest payments on your main residence or holiday home

- claiming interest payments for properties that are not genuinely available for rent

- incorrectly apportioning interest deductions for loans that are partly investments and partly private and domestic—incidentally, this is normally done on an area basis (see chapter 5)

- claiming a deduction for interest payments throughout the year when a property is only rented out for part of the year.

 Tax tip

If you use your main residence as collateral to secure a loan to buy a rental property the interest

Tax tip (*cont'd*)

you incur is tax deductible, as the purpose of the loan is to derive assessable income (namely rent). But if you did the opposite and used your rental property as collateral to secure a loan to buy your main residence, the interest you incur is not tax deductible. This is because the purpose of the loan is to buy a non-income-producing property (namely your main residence). Incidentally, the security you offer to get a loan is irrelevant as to whether you can or cannot claim a tax deduction.

 Tax trap

If you have a split loan facility where part of the loan is used to repay your home mortgage and part of the loan is used to buy a rental property, you'll need to keep separate details of the arrangement. There are certain tax rules for claiming interest deductions under a split loan arrangement. For more details see the Tax Office publication *Split loan interest deductions*. You can download a copy from the Tax Office website <www.ato.gov.au>. See also appendix A, Split loan facilities.

Borrowing costs

Under Australian tax law, you can claim a tax deduction for 'expenditure incurred for borrowing money to the extent that the money is used for the purposes of gaining or producing assessable income' (for instance, rent). If your borrowing expenses (for instance, loan establishment fees, legal expenses, stamp duty on the mortgage, valuation and survey fees) do not exceed $100, you can claim the amount outright in the financial year you incur them. But if they exceed this amount, as is usually the case, you'll need to spread your total borrowing expenses over the period of the loan or over five years (or 1826 days to be precise) if your loan exceeds the five-year limit. Incidentally, the Tax Office points out that a common mistake relating to borrowing costs is incorrectly claiming the full amount in the financial year they're incurred, rather than over the term of the loan, or five years (see chapter 9).

The following formula is used to apportion the amount of borrowing expenses you can legally claim each financial year:

Borrowing costs × Period in year ÷ Total period of loan (maximum five years).

Case study: claiming borrowing costs

On 1 November 2011 Franca takes out a 10-year loan to buy a rental property. The borrowing costs associated with setting up the loan amount to $4000. As the purpose of the loan is to buy a rental property the borrowing costs are tax-deductible expenses. Because the total borrowing costs exceed $100, Franca needs to spread the $4000 she incurs over the period of the loan, or over five years (1826 days) if the loan exceeds five years. In this case the loan is over 10 years and Franca must apportion the $4000 in borrowing costs over five years (more particularly 1826 days), as illustrated in table 7.1.

Table 7.1: apportioning borrowing costs

2011–12 Yr	$532	($4000 × 243 days ÷ 1826 days)
2012–13 Yr	$800	
2013–14 Yr	$800	
2014–15 Yr	$800	
2015–16 Yr	$800	
2016–17 Yr	$270	(the balance of the tax deduction)

Note: If you take out a loan part way through a financial year (for instance, 1 November 2011), you'll need to apportion a pro-rata amount to claim in the first financial year that you incur the borrowing costs.

 Tax tip

The Tax Office has advised that the costs associated with the transfer of title when you buy a rental property (such as the stamp duty on transfer, land titles office fee and registration of title fee) are not part of the borrowing costs. These transfer costs may form part of the property's cost base for capital gains tax purposes (see chapter 4).

At a glance: choosing a loan to buy a property

There are many types of loans for purchasing a property. The common ones are listed here:

- *Principal and interest loans:* For these loans, you'll need to pay back both the interest and principal at regular intervals (for instance, on a fortnightly basis). Note: only the interest component is tax deductible (provided the loan is for the purposes of deriving assessable income). Your principal repayments are capital in nature and not tax deductible.

- *Interest-only loans:* You're only required to repay the interest you incur with this type of loan. The principal is repaid at a later date or when the loan matures.

- *Home loans:* This kind of loan is used to buy your main residence. The loan may have certain features tailored to suit your personal needs; for instance, a redraw facility or line of credit where you can access additional funds to buy a rental property.

- *Split loans:* This is a loan that is partly a home loan and partly an investment loan. If you plan to take out a split loan there are special tax rules you'll need to follow when claiming the interest payments as a tax-deductible expense.

- *Line of credit loans:* With this facility you can access money up to an approved predetermined limit. You'll normally offer your main residence as collateral to secure a loan that can be as much as 85 per cent of the value of your property. These loans allow you to access the necessary funds to buy a rental property.

- *Bridging loans:* These are short-term loans to cover you while you're finalising a financial transaction. For instance, you may need funds to buy a new property now while you're waiting to receive the proceeds from a property you have recently sold.

- *Low-doc loans:* For these loans, no documentary evidence is required to verify your capacity to service the loan repayments. They're normally offered to high-risk investors at a high rate of interest. There's a possibility you could forfeit your security (for instance property) if you're unable to meet your loan repayments.

- *Vendor finance loans:* In this case, the vendor (for instance, the property developer) provides you with the necessary finance to purchase a property.

Wealth creation: key tax-planning issues

There are three key tax-planning issues you'll need take on board if you intend to borrow money to buy a rental property to help build up your wealth. They are:

- investment growth potential

- derivation of rent

- capacity to claim a tax deduction.

Investment growth potential

When you borrow money to buy a rental property, you'll be hoping that the property will appreciate in value over time. From an investment perspective rental properties tend to yield about 4 per cent per annum. When you take the various annual expenses you're likely to incur (such as council rates, land taxes, insurance and repairs) and the payment of income tax, the net yield is generally around the 2 per cent per annum mark. So it's essential that your property is capable of generating capital growth to make this a viable investment option. Otherwise, you will be financing the purchase of an investment asset that won't make you wealthy in the long term.

As a rule of thumb properties in good locations tend to double in value every seven to ten years. Under Australian tax law any unrealised capital growth is not liable to tax until the property is sold. And to add icing to the investment cake, if you keep the property for more than 12 months, only 50 per cent of any realised capital gain you make on the sale is taxable. The balance is exempt and excluded from your assessable income (see Case study: negative gearing a rental property on p. 138).

Derivation of rent

Make sure you charge your tenants a commercial rate of rent. Otherwise, there is a strong possibility that the

Tax Office will disallow your tax deductions or reduce them to an amount that's considered reasonable; see appendix A, Apportionment of rental deductions. This could become a major concern if you plan to lease your property to a family member for a nominal amount of rent (for instance, $10 per week).

On the other hand, if your property is temporarily vacant, make sure it's genuinely available for rent at a commercial rate, in order to continue to claim a tax deduction for any expenditure you incur. For example, the property should be listed with a real estate agent and/or you're advertising to find a suitable tenant (see chapter 3).

Capacity to claim a tax deduction

Remember, your capacity to claim a tax deduction is dependent on whether you are deriving assessable income (such as salary and wages, business profits and investment income). Otherwise, you may lose the opportunity to claim any net rental losses you incur. This will arise if your taxable income is below $16 000, as you can claim a low income tax offset (see Negative gearing).

Negative gearing

A major investment strategy linked with borrowing money to buy a rental property is negative gearing. Negative gearing is often promoted by property developers to entice you to buy a new property from them.

This is how negative gearing works. If your total rental expenses (for instance, interest payments, depreciation, council rates, insurance and repairs) exceed the gross rent you receive, you can deduct the net rental loss you incur from other assessable income you derive (such as salary and wages, business profits and investment income). When you do this you'll save paying tax on the assessable income you derive from other sources!

Incidentally, back in the 1980s the federal government introduced legislation to restrict your ability to negative gear a rental property, with disastrous effects. The legislation was repelled a few years later when construction of new property developments started to decline, and landlords began to increase the rent on existing properties as a consequence.

From a tax-planning point of view negative gearing will significantly benefit high-income earners, as the potential tax savings will be much greater. For example, if your marginal rate of tax is 30 per cent you stand to save 30 cents for every dollar you claim as a tax deduction, compared with 15 cents if your marginal rate of tax is 15 per cent. This will be the case if your taxable income is below $37 000. But if your taxable income were to fall below $16 000 your ability to claim a tax deduction is effectively lost, as no tax is payable once your taxable income falls below this amount (as you can claim a low income tax offset). As you are effectively losing money while you're negative gearing, it's important that your property is appreciating in value to counter the net loss you're incurring while paying off the loan. Otherwise, you could find yourself buying a property that's both decreasing in value and generating a negative cash inflow!

 Tax tip

For the Tax Office's views on negative gearing you can read 'Tax Office Ruling TR 95/33 Income tax: subsection 51(1) — relevance of subjective purpose, motive or intention in determining the deductibility of losses and outgoings'.

Case study: negative gearing a rental property

Seven years ago Jonathon borrowed $350 000 (at 8 per cent per annum) to purchase a rental property. The purchase price was $500 000. At the time of purchase he was advised the building's construction costs were $300 000. As the building was constructed after September 1987 Jonathon can claim a 2.5 per cent per annum capital-works deduction (see chapter 3). For the current financial year, the amount of salary and wages he derived was $70 000 and his marginal rate of tax plus the Medicare levy is 31.5 per cent.

At the end of the financial year Jonathan's accounting records provided the following information:

⇒ gross rent received: $20 000

⇒ interest payments on loan: $28 000

⇒ annual rental deductions (council rates and land taxes, insurance and repairs): $3 000

⇒ depreciation deductions: $4 500

⇒ capital-works deduction: $7500 ($300 000 × 2.5%)

⇒ current market value of the property: $1 000 000.

Calculating the net rental loss

Gross rent received		$20 000
Less:		
Deductible expenses:		
Interest payments on loan	$28 000	
Annual rental expenditure	$3 000	
Depreciation deduction	$4 500	
Capital works deduction	$7 500	$43 000
Net rental loss		$23 000

As Jonathon has incurred a $23 000 net rental loss from negative gearing his rental property, the loss can be deducted from the $70 000 salary and wages he derived from his employment activities as illustrated here.

Salary and wages	$70 000
Less:	
Net loss from rent	$23 000
Taxable income	$47 000

As Jonathon's marginal rate of tax (plus the Medicare levy) is 31.5 per cent, when the net rental loss is deducted from his salary and wages, he will gain a tax saving amounting to $7245 ($23 000 × 31.5% = $7245). When Jonathon adds up all his total cash inflows (rent and tax saving) and deducts the amount from all his cash outflows (cash expenses), the shortfall

Jonathon will need to fund from his personal savings is only $3755 (or $72 per week) as illustrated below.

Cash flow statement

Cash inflow:

Gross rent	$20 000	
Tax saved	$7 245	$27 245

Cash outflow:

Interest payments	$28 000	
Rental expenditure	$3 000	$31 000
Net cash outlay		$3 755

(Note: as the depreciation deductions and capital-works deductions are merely book entries and not actual cash outlays, they are not included in the cash flow statement as illustrated above).

So for a net cash outlay of $72 per week, Jonathon is paying off a rental property that has doubled in value from $500 000 to $1 000 000 over a seven-year period. An extra advantage is that the $500 000 in unrealised capital growth is not liable to tax until the property is subsequently sold. In this case, as Jonathon has owned the property for more than 12 months, only 50 per cent of any realised capital gain he makes on sale is taxable. The balance is exempt and excluded from his assessable income (see chapter 4).

Paying the correct market price

If you're planning on buying a new property from a property developer using the benefits of negative gearing to finance the purchase, make sure that you don't pay more than the property is worth. Keep in mind the property developer's sale price may not necessarily reflect the property's market value. This is often a trap for novice investors. To avoid any potential pitfalls, before you sign on the dotted line, it's best to get an independent opinion — it's better to be safe than sorry! Otherwise, you could find yourself paying thousands of dollars more that its market value.

 Tax tip

The Tax Office has advised that if your rental expenses are likely to exceed the gross rent, you can reduce the rate of tax payable on other assessable income you derive such as your salary and wages. To do this you'll need to complete the form 'PAYG income tax withholding variation (ITWV) application (NAT 2036)'. You can download a copy from the Tax Office website <www.ato.gov.au>.

Positive gearing

From an investment perspective it is best if you can positive gear. Positive gearing means the rent you receive (cash inflow) covers all your rental expenses (cash outflow). This means apart from any initial funds you may have contributed, your tenant is effectively financing the balance of the purchase price on your behalf! The bonus here is that if your property is appreciating in value while you're paying off the loan, you will receive a cash inflow (plus capital growth that's not taxable until the property is sold), without using any of your own money to service the loan repayments.

Case study: positive gearing a rental property

Four years ago Anthony paid $350 000 for a rental property. He used $50 000 of his own money and took out a $300 000 interest-only loan to finance the balance of the purchase price. At the end of the financial year he had received $25 000 gross rent and his rental expenses (predominantly interest payments) were $23 000. As Anthony's cash inflows ($25 000) exceeded his cash outflows ($23 000) he is positive gearing, which means his tenant is effectively funding the loan repayments on his behalf. His real estate agent has advised him the property has appreciated $200 000 in value since he originally bought it. Anthony is deriving a $2000 positive cash inflow plus $200 000 capital growth without using his own money to service the loan repayments!

Useful references

- FIDO, the consumer website of the Australian Securities & Investments Commission, <www.fido.gov.au> — go to 'About financial products' then click 'Borrowing and credit'

Australian Taxation Office publications

- *Rental properties (NAT 1729)* — go to the section 'Interest on loans'

Australian Taxation Office interpretative decisions

- ID 2006/297: *Income tax: deductibility of compound interest on a split loan facility*

Other taxation rulings

- TR 2000/2: *Income tax: deductibility of interest on moneys drawn down under line of credit facilities and redraw facilities*

- IT 2684: *Income tax: deductibility of interest on money borrowed to acquire units in a property unit trust*

- TA 2001/1: *Home loan unit trust arrangement*

- TA 2008/3: *Uncommercial use of certain trusts*

Chapter 8

Six legal ways of owning property: this is how you're taxed

Investing in real estate is not just a simple matter of finding a suitable property in a good location and signing the contract of sale. You'll also need to be aware of the different legal ways that you can own a property. This is important to know as there are a number of taxation and commercial advantages (as well as limitations) associated with owning property under a particular legal structure that you'll need to weigh up. As you'll be paying a substantial sum to buy a property, it's best that you seek professional advice from a financial planner, solicitor and/or tax consultant. In this chapter I examine the ownership options and point out the unique tax issues that could influence your decision (see table 8.1, overleaf).

Table 8.1: comparing ownership structures

Legal structure	Main-residence exemption	CGT discount	Distribute income	Distribute losses	Tax rates	Split income/ losses
Individual	Yes	Yes	Yes	Yes	Marginal	No
Co-owners	Yes	Yes	Yes	Yes	Marginal	Yes
Company	No	No	Yes	No	30%	Income only
Trust	No	Yes	Yes	No	Marginal	Income only
Property trust	No	Yes	Yes	No	Marginal	Income only
Superannuation	No	Yes	No	No	15%	No

The six most common ways of owning a property are:

- outright ownership
- co-ownership (partnership)
- company
- trust
- property trust
- self managed superannuation fund.

At a glance: legal structures and taxation

Owning property under the six common legal structures will affect:

- your capacity to access certain capital gains tax concessions
- the rate of tax you're liable to pay under the different legal structures
- the number of tax deductions you can claim each year
- your capacity to split assessable income, such as rental income, and allowable deductions with family members
- your capacity to claim tax losses you may incur each financial year (especially if you're planning to negative gear your property purchases, see chapter 7).

Outright ownership: this property belongs to me

If the rental property is under your name you will own the property outright, which means you get to keep all the net income and any potential capital growth. Under Australian tax law the rental income you receive is liable to tax at your marginal rates of tax (which can vary between 0 per cent and 45 per cent), and you can claim all the allowable deductions you incur. This is a significant benefit to have up your sleeve if you plan to negative gear, as you can immediately deduct your net rental losses against other assessable income you derive (see chapter 7). You'll also be liable to pay capital gains tax (CGT) if you sell the property and make a capital gain.

But the good news here is that an individual can claim a 50 per cent CGT discount if the property is owned for more than 12 months. But wait, there's more—if the property happens to be your main residence, it will be exempt from CGT! On the other hand, if you make a capital loss, you can deduct the capital loss from a current or future capital gain you make on the sale of other CGT assets that you own. In contrast, losses within a company or trust structure cannot be distributed (and these legal structures cannot claim a main-residence exemption); see table 8.1.

A major limitation of outright ownership is your inability to split any rental income you derive or capital gains you make on sale with family members (see table 8.1). This is also the case if you decide to gift or transfer ownership to someone else (for instance, to a family member or to your self managed superannuation fund).

At a glance: how individuals are taxed

Under Australian tax law, individuals:

- must apply for a tax file number (TFN) and lodge an annual tax return

- pay tax on a progressive basis at their marginal rates of tax (which can vary between 0 per cent and 45 per cent), but the first $6000 earned is tax-free

- are liable to pay a 1.5 per cent Medicare levy

- are liable to pay CGT at their marginal rates of tax, but they can claim a 50 per cent CGT discount if they own a property for more than 12 months

- can only deduct capital losses from capital gains

- may qualify for certain tax offsets (for instance, a low income tax offset and spouse tax offset)

- pay no tax if their taxable income falls below $16000 (as you can claim the low income tax offset)

- can claim a main-residence exemption.

 Tax tip

Ordinarily if you co-own a property you will either own it as 'joint tenants' (for instance, husband and

Tax tip *(cont'd)*

wife) or 'tenants in common' (for instance, business partners or relatives). If the property is co-owned as 'joint tenants' and one joint tenant dies, their legal interest in the property will automatically pass to the surviving joint tenant. Incidentally, if the property is a pre-CGT property, the surviving joint tenant will now own a 50 per cent pre-CGT property and a 50 per cent post-CGT property. On the other hand, if a property is owned as 'tenants in common' and one person dies, their legal interest in the property can be transferred to a nominated beneficiary. Under the CGT provisions death does not trigger a CGT event, which means no CGT liability will arise at the time of death.

Co-ownership (partnership)

Under Australia tax law if you co-own a rental property as joint tenants or tenants in common you will be considered to be in partnership. The Tax Act defines a partnership to include 'an association of persons in receipt of ordinary income or statutory income jointly' (such as rental income and capital gains). Technically speaking, if you're in partnership, you'll need apply for a partnership TFN and lodge a partnership tax return disclosing the partnership net income or partnership net loss. Under tax law a partnership is not liable to pay tax on the partnership net income it derives, as all net income (or net losses) must be distributed to the individual partners.

This means you're only liable to pay tax on your share of the distribution of net partnership income.

But the good news here is that if you're merely deriving investment income jointly (such as interest, dividends and rent) you're not obligated to apply for a partnership TFN, nor lodge a partnership tax return. But you are required to disclose your share of any partnership investment income (or loss) in your individual tax return.

Under the CGT provisions partnership assets (such as a co-owned rental property) are proportionally owned by each partner in accordance with their respective partnership interest. This means any capital gains or capital losses you make on disposal are proportionally derived by each partner, and each of you must disclose it in your respective individual tax returns. Further, individual partners are eligible to claim a 50 per cent CGT discount on sale of CGT assets (such as property) owned for more than 12 months. Incidentally, this is not the case if a property is owned in a company structure (see table 8.1).

A major advantage of co-owning a rental property is the ability to split any net rental income among the joint owners in accordance with their legal interest in the property. If you're not carrying on a rental property business and own the rental property as joint tenants, the split is ordinarily done on a 50–50 basis. On the other hand, if you own the rental property as tenants in common the split is ordinarily done in accordance with your legal interest in the property. This is also the case with net rental losses. Your capacity to access losses is an important concept if you're negative gearing, as each partner can immediately deduct their share of any net distributed rental losses from other assessable income they derive. By the way, this is not the case if a rental property is owned in a company or trust structure, as these legal entities are prohibited from distributing losses (see table 8.1).

 Tax tip

The Tax Office has advised in its publication *Rental properties (NAT 1729)* that if 'you carry on a rental property business in partnership with others, you must divide the net rental income or loss according to the partnership agreement', and that you must do this 'whether or not the legal interests in the rental properties are different to the partners' entitlements to profits and losses under the partnership agreement'.

A major limitation under a partnership structure is that a partnership can't distribute all the net partnership income or net partnership loss to one partner and nothing to the other. This is because if you're not carrying on a rental property business, all partnership distributions must be made in accordance to each partner's legal interest in the property. The fact that it may be set out in a formal partnership agreement that you can do this is irrelevant under tax law; see appendix A, Co-owned rental property.

At a glance: how partnerships are taxed

Under Australian tax law, a partnership (and more particularly partnerships receiving rental income jointly):

- is not liable to pay tax, but individual partners must disclose their share of any net partnership income (net rent) in their individual tax returns

- doesn't need to lodge a partnership tax return (if receiving income jointly), nor apply for a partnership TFN

- can distribute net partnership losses to individual partners

- holds assets (co-owned property) that are proportionally owned by each partner

- allows individual partners to claim a 50 per cent CGT discount on sale of co-owned property owned for more than 12 months.

Company

Under corporations law a company is a separate legal entity. This means it has an independent existence from its shareholders and can own, buy and sell investment assets such as real estate. Under Australian tax law a company pays tax at the rate of 30 per cent on every dollar of net profit it derives. Incidentally, the federal government has proposed reducing this rate to 29 per cent in 2013–14.

From an investment and tax-planning point of view, there are a number of disadvantages to using a company structure for owning investment assets such as real estate (see table 8.1). This is especially the case if you set up a private company. The main disadvantages are listed here.

- Companies cannot distribute company losses to their shareholders. Company losses must remain within the company structure and can only be deducted from future company profits. This could be a major nuisance if a company is negative gearing an investment property and accumulating substantial tax losses that cannot be distributed to shareholders (see chapter 7).

- Under the CGT provisions companies are ineligible for the 50 per cent CGT discount (see chapter 4). This is not great news if the property increases substantially in value, as the entire capital gain on sale will be taxed at the rate of 30 per cent.

- Companies cannot distribute company profits (referred to as dividends) to specific shareholders. Dividend distributions must be made in proportion to the number of shares you own. For example, if you own 50 per cent of the shares in a company, you will receive 50 per cent of any dividend distribution the company declares.

- Although a company has the benefit of limited liability (meaning the shareholders' liability is limited to the value of their shares in the company), company directors may need to give personal guarantees for company loans (for instance, to buy a rental property).

- A private company that owns assets such as a rental property must charge a commercial rate of rent if the property is made available to shareholders or their associates (such as a shareholder's relative). Otherwise, the Tax Office may treat the benefit derived as a deemed dividend and liable to tax.

 Tax trap

The Tax Office has issued a ruling pointing out that a company is ineligible to claim a main-residence exemption in a property that it owns. This is the case even if the directors reside in the property. Under Australian tax law only an individual and, more particularly, a natural person can reside in and own a main residence.

At a glance: how companies are taxed

Under Australian tax law, a company:

- must apply for a TFN and lodge an annual company tax return

- pays a flat 30 per cent rate of tax on the entire amount of taxable income it derives; it misses out on the $6000 tax-free threshold that's available to individuals

- can't claim certain domestic tax offsets (such as a low income tax offset)

- doesn't have to distribute profits (dividends) to shareholders; the profits can remain within the company structure, and the company can decide when to make a distribution

- can't stream dividends to specific shareholders

- can't distribute losses to shareholders; there are stringent rules regulating private companies claiming prior-year losses

- can't claim a 50 per cent CGT discount

- can't claim a main-residence exemption.

Trust structure

A trust is a legal obligation binding a person (the trustee) with beneficial use and control over investment assets (for instance, a residential property) for the benefit of beneficiaries. There are a number of advantages to owning a rental property under a trust structure (and more particularly a family discretionary trust) that may appeal to you. For example, if a family trust owns a rental property, the trustee can lease the property to the beneficiaries of the trust and benefit from negative gearing (see chapter 7). By the way, this is on the condition that the trustee charges a commercial rate of rent; see appendix A, Trusts (and negative gearing).

Under a family discretionary trust arrangement, the trustee can decide how the trust net income (such as net rent and capital gains) should be distributed to the beneficiaries, who are normally family members. A major advantage of operating a trust is that a trustee can nominate which beneficiary should receive a trust distribution, and the amount they should receive (see Case study: receiving a trust distribution on p. 160).

In contrast, under a partnership or company structure, the distribution must be made in accordance with the respective legal entitlements. No tax is payable if your taxable income is below $16 000 (per 2010–11 tax rates), as you can claim a low income tax offset. So from a tax-planning point of view, a trustee can effectively distribute to beneficiaries whose taxable income is below this amount. However, there are anti-avoidance provisions to discourage a trustee from distributing unearned income (such as net rental income) to beneficiaries who are under 18 years of age. This is because distributions to minor beneficiaries are taxed at a special rate (see table 8.2). As minor beneficiaries can claim a low income tax offset (currently $1500), the trustee can effectively distribute up to $3333 (per 2010–11 tax rates) before this special rate of tax will apply.

But there are certain disadvantages that you'll need to take on board if you intend to use a trust structure. They arise

Table 8.2: distribution to minors—special rate of tax

Taxable income	Rate of tax
$0–416	Nil tax payable
$417–1445	66% of excess over $416
Above $1445	45% on entire amount of taxable income

because a trust can't distribute net losses to beneficiaries. As is the case with companies, trust losses must remain within the trust structure and can only be offset against future trust income. There are also stringent provisions you'll need to satisfy to claim trust losses. For more details see the Tax Office publication *Family trust elections and interposed entity elections—trust loss measures questions and answers*. As is the case with a company structure, this could be a major concern if a trust is negative gearing a rental property and accumulating substantial tax losses that cannot be distributed to the beneficiaries (see chapter 7).

 Tax tip

Income flowing through a trust will retain its identity or character when a trustee makes a trust distribution to beneficiaries. This means that if a trustee were to distribute rental income or a capital gain that qualifies for a 50 per cent CGT discount, it will still be rental income or a capital gain that qualifies for a 50 per cent CGT discount in the hands of the individual beneficiaries.

 Tax trap

The Tax Office has issued a ruling pointing out that a trust is not entitled to claim a main-residence exemption. This is the case even if the trustee uses the premises as their main residence.

At a glance: how trusts are taxed

Under Australian tax law, a trust:

- must apply for a trust TFN and lodge a trust tax return disclosing the trust net income (or trust net loss)

- is not liable to pay tax on the trust net income it derives; trust net income is assessed to either the trustee or beneficiaries, such that:

  - if a beneficiary is presently entitled to a trust distribution (meaning they have a legal right to demand payment), the income is assessed to them

  - if a beneficiary is presently entitled but is under a legal disability (for instance, he or she is a minor or mentally incompetent), the trustee is liable to pay the tax

  - if no beneficiary is presently entitled or the trustee decides not to make a trust distribution, the trustee is ordinarily liable to pay tax at the rate of 45 per cent (plus a Medicare levy)

- can't distribute trust losses to beneficiaries; there are stringent rules regulating trusts claiming prior-year losses

- can lease a rental property to its beneficiaries provided the trustee charges a commercial rate of rent.

Case study: receiving a trust distribution

According to the accounts of the Robinson family discretionary trust, the trustee received the following amounts from the trust's property investment holdings:

Gross rent	$38 000
Less:	
Deductible rental expenses	$6 000
Net trust income	$32 000

At the end of the financial year the trustee resolved to distribute the trust net income to the following beneficiaries:

⇒ $15 000 to Angela, who is 20 years of age and in full-time education. This is her sole source of income

⇒ $14 000 to Richard, who is 19 years of age and in full-time education. This is his sole source of income

⇒ $3000 to Olivia, who is two years of age.

Distribution to Angela ($15 000)

As Angela is over 18 years of age, she is presently entitled to the trust distribution and is under no legal disability. As her total taxable income is below $16 000 no tax is payable on this amount.

Distribution to Richard ($14 000)

As Richard is over 18 years of age, he is presently entitled to the trust distribution and is under no legal disability. As his total taxable income is below $16000 no tax is payable as this amount.

Distribution to Olivia ($3000)

As Olivia is presently entitled to the trust distribution but is under a legal disability (being a beneficiary under 18 years of age), the trustee is liable to pay tax on this distribution. As the amount distributed is less than $3333, no tax is payable on this amount.

So under this structure the trustee as effectively distributed $32000 among the family members and no tax is payable!

 Tax trap

Beneficiaries of family discretionary trusts need to supply their individual tax file numbers to the trustee. Otherwise, the trustee must withhold tax at the rate of 46.5 per cent from the payment. For more details see the Tax Office publication *TFN withholding for closely held trusts*.

Property trust

Property trusts are managed (or pooled) investment funds that invest predominantly in major residential, shopping and commercial property developments located throughout Australia and/or overseas. Professional fund managers are responsible for buying and selling properties and managing the trust's property portfolio. Property trusts normally enter into long-term leases and pay regular income distributions to their unit holders. The yield is generally about 6 per cent to 8 per cent per annum. In return for management services, investors incur ongoing fees and charges.

Investing in a property trust gives small investors and self managed superannuation fund members who can't afford to buy a property outright the opportunity to invest in property. It also gives investors who would prefer to maintain a diversified investment portfolio some exposure to the property market.

When you invest in a property trust you purchase units. As with shares, the value of your units will rise and fall on a daily basis in line with the prevailing property market. As this type of investment is a long-term strategy, you may need to wait many years for your units to increase significantly in value. But there is a risk that they could also fall in value.

You can invest in listed property trusts, which are listed on the Australian Securities Exchange (ASX), and unlisted property trusts, which are not listed on the ASX. A major advantage of listed property trusts is that you can quickly buy and sell your units on the ASX in the same way you buy and sell shares. Many of Australia's leading property trusts are listed on the ASX. Property trusts listed in the S&P/ASX 200 index include:

- BWP   Bunning Warehouse Property Trusts
- CFX   CFS Retail Property Trust

- CPA   Commonwealth Property Office Fund

- GMG   Goodman Group

- GPT   GPT Group

- IIF   ING Industrial Fund

- MCW   Macquarie Countrywide Trust

- MGR   Mirvac Group

- SGP   Stockland

- WDC   Westfield Group.

On the other hand, if you want to invest in an unlisted property trust you'll need to contact the trustee directly and fill out a product disclosure statement. This legal document will set out relevant information about the trust's property holdings, the risks you're taking, plus the various ongoing management fees and charges you will incur.

 Tax tip

If you plan to borrow money to invest in a property trust, some of your interest payments may not be tax deductible. For more information you can read TR IT 2684 *Deductibility of interest on money borrowed to acquire units in a property unit trust*. You can download a copy from the Tax Office website <www.ato.gov.au>.

When assessing which property trust to invest your money with you'll need to consider questions such as:

- What kind of properties does the trust hold, and where are they located?

- Are property valuations realistic?

- How much debt is the property trust carrying, and can it adequately service the debt repayments from the revenue it derives?

- How could current economic conditions affect property valuations and yields?

- Who are the tenants (for instance federal or state government agencies)?

- When are the property leases due to expire?

- Are any properties currently vacant (which could adversely affect profits)?

- Is there any major refurbishment taking place (which could adversely affect profits)?

- Is the net profit the property trust derives each year growing or falling?

- What is the property trust's policy around paying assessable distributions and non-assessable distributions (see figure 8.1)?

- What are the ongoing management fees and charges you're likely to incur?

Figure 8.1: property trust distributions

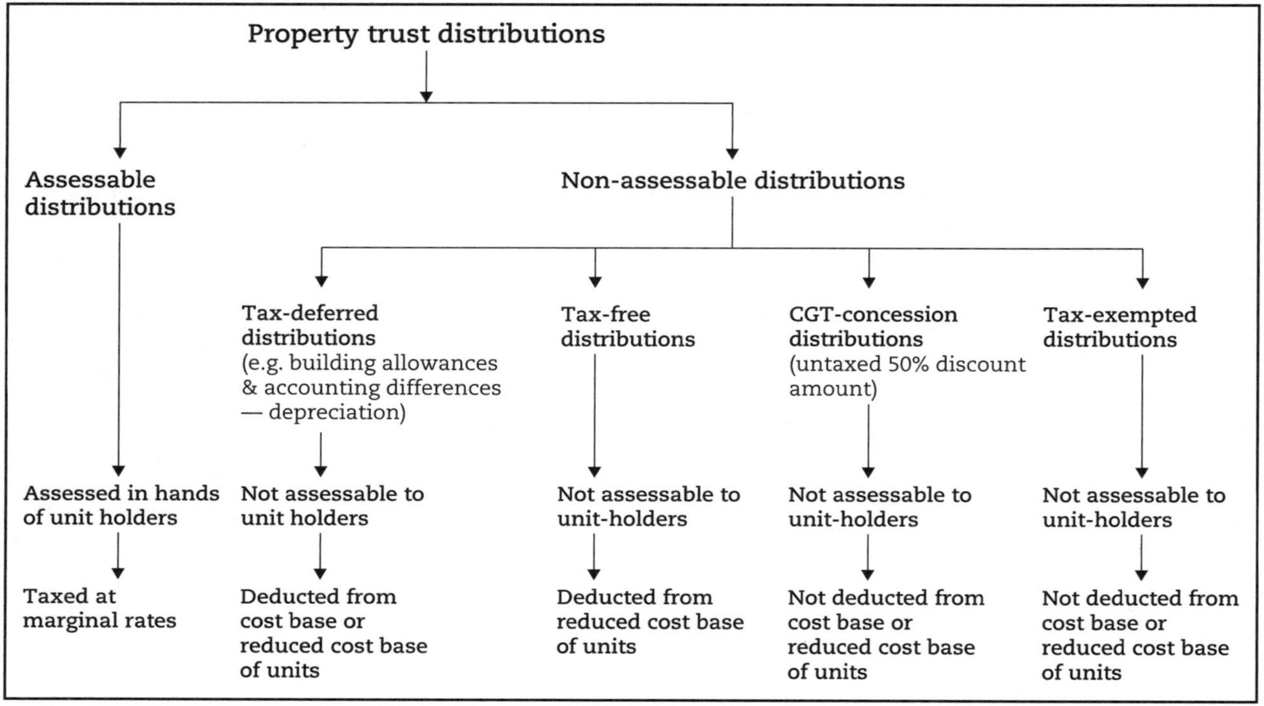

At a glance: how property trusts are taxed

Property trusts normally make two types of distributions to unit holders—assessable distributions and non-assessable distributions (see figure 8.1).

- *Assessable distributions* such as rental receipts are liable to tax at your marginal rates.

- *Non-assessable distributions* are not assessable to unit holders; more particularly, under the CGT provisions:

  □ *tax-deferred distributions* are deducted from the unit's cost base or reduced cost base

  □ *tax-free distributions* are deducted from the unit's reduced cost base when calculating a capital loss

  □ *CGT-concession distributions* are not deducted from the unit's cost base or reduced cost base

  □ *tax-exempted distributions* are not deducted from the cost base or reduced cost base.

When you sell your units you could make a capital gain or capital loss.

 Tax trap

A major headache with this form of investing is that you have to constantly adjust the unit's cost base when you receive certain trust distributions, which means you have to keep accurate records and know

how to make the relevant adjustments. It can be costly having to regularly consult a tax agent to make these potential ongoing adjustments for you.

Self managed superannuation fund

Superannuation is an investment vehicle that allows you to buy wealth-creating assets (such as shares and real estate) that you can access when you reach your preservation age and retire. Under current legislation your preservation age is 55 years of age if you're born before 1960, and 60 years of age if you're born after 1964. You need to adjust your age if you happen to be born between these two dates.

One option you can consider is to set up and manage your own complying self managed superannuation fund (SMSF). It's called a complying fund because you must elect to be regulated (for instance, by the Australian Taxation Office) and comply with the *Superannuation Industry (Supervision) Act 1993*. A significant benefit of running your own super fund is that you can choose your own investment strategy to help fund your retirement (for instance, buy a number of rental properties and/or invest in property trusts).

Over the years the federal government has introduced a number of incentives to encourage you to continually put money into a superannuation fund. One such incentive is that once you reach 60 years of age and retire, all withdrawals when your superannuation fund is in the pension phase are exempt from tax. This is great news if your SMSF happens to own a number of properties that have appreciated substantially in value, as no tax is payable!

From a tax-planning point of view, as property has the capacity to appreciate in value, it can be an ideal investment option to help boost your retirement nest egg. And when you take on board the fact that no tax is payable once you reach 60 years of age and your super fund is in the pension phase — what more can one say but yippee!

But you can't access your benefits until you satisfy a condition of release, such as by retiring. This can be a bit of a nuisance if you want to retire early and you've got a truckload of money sitting in your super fund that you can't immediately access. Unfortunately, this is the price you have to pay if you want to use a superannuation fund to help build up your wealth.

 Tax trap

The Tax Office has issued a ruling pointing out that the fees for setting up a SMSF are capital in nature and are not tax-deductible expenses.

At a glance: how complying superannuation funds are taxed

Under Australian tax law, a complying superannuation fund:

- must apply for a superannuation fund TFN and lodge a superannuation fund tax return each year

- pays tax at the rate of 15 per cent

- is liable to a 15 per cent tax on only two-thirds of a capital gain on the sale of investment assets held for more than 12 months (for instance, a property) — this means the entire capital gain is effectively taxed at the rate of 10 per cent.

If you invest in a complying superannuation fund:

- all pensions and cash withdrawals payable once you turn 60 years of age and retire are exempt from tax

- any income and capital gains your super fund derives (during the pension phase of your super fund) to fund your pension payments are exempt from tax, which means all capital gains on the sale of investment assets such as property are excluded from assessable income!

- you can take advantage of tax incentives; for instance, if you're self-employed your contributions are tax deductible, while low income earners may qualify for a number of government concessions.

 Tax trap

A major limitation on putting money into super is that you can't access your benefits until you reach your preservation age and retire. If you're born before 1960 you can access your benefits once you reach 55 years of age, or 60 years of age if you're born after 1964.

The rules you'll need to follow

Once you set up your own SMSF and agree to be regulated you'll need to comply with the following rules.

- The sole purpose of setting up a SMSF must be to provide benefits to members upon retirement and benefits to dependants in the event of a member's death. This means you cannot reside in a property that is owned by your super fund.

- Ordinarily a SMSF is prohibited from borrowing money to purchase investment assets such as property unless certain conditions are met (see Borrowing to buy a property on p. 174).

- You can't use your fund's assets as a guarantee to secure a loan.

- You must prepare an investment strategy setting out the investments you intend to buy (for instance, a property) and the risks you will be taking. For more details see the Tax Office publication *Investment strategy*.

- You must appoint an independent auditor to verify that your SMSF is a complying super fund. Your fund must be audited by an approved auditor each financial year and prior to lodging your annual super fund tax return.

Note: if you fail to comply with these rules there's a risk that the Tax Office could treat your SMSF as a non-complying super fund. If this occurs you will lose certain tax concessions available to members, and the fund will be liable to pay tax at the rate of 45 per cent.

 Tax tip

A SMSF can own a property as tenants in common with another entity and can own units in a unit trust that owns a property. This is on the proviso that the super fund's interest in the property can't be at risk.

 Tax trap

You can't sell or transfer a residential property that you own to your SMSF. If you did this you would contravene the Superannuation Industry (Supervision) Act.

Owning property in a superannuation fund

A SMSF can purchase and own property (such as a commercial or residential property) in its own right. As property is generally regarded as a long-term investment strategy, owning property in a SMSF could prove a great investment strategy if the property appreciates in value during the accumulation phase of the fund.

However, a major risk with owning property in a SMSF is that you may experience difficulty selling it at short notice. This is especially so if there are no willing buyers who are prepared to pay the selling price you're asking. This could turn into a minor disaster if the super fund's investments are predominantly tied up in real estate, and you need to realise a substantial amount of cash immediately to pay out a member who has retired, or to a member's beneficiary in the event of death.

Business real property

If you operate your own business, a SMSF can purchase your business premises (referred to as business real property) at market value, and lease it back to you at a commercial rate of rent. Under the CGT provisions if you sell or transfer your business premises (for instance, your office or factory) to your SMSF, you could be liable to pay CGT on any capital gain you make at the time the property is sold or transferred to your super fund. This is because your SMSF will now own the property. However, all is not lost because if you run a small business, you may qualify for CGT relief under the CGT concessions for small business provisions. By the way, under Australian tax law you're considered to be running a small business if your annual turnover (sales) is less than $2 million per annum. For more details see the Tax Office publication *Concessions for small business entities—overview (NAT 71398)*.

Further, depending on your state or territory, your super fund may be liable to pay stamp duty at the time of sale or transfer. But you may be eligible for concessions or exemptions if you satisfy certain conditions. For more details you can visit your local state or territory government revenue office website (see chapter 5).

From a tax-planning point of view if your SMSF owns your business premises, once you turn 60 years of age and retire, any capital gain your super fund makes on the sale of the business premises during the super fund's pension phase is exempt from tax.

For more details you can read the Tax Office publications *What does business real property mean?* and *SMSFR 2009/1 Self Managed Superannuation Funds: business real property for the purposes of the Superannuation Industry (Supervision) Act 1993.* You can download a copy from the Tax Office website.

 Tax trap

If you plan to transfer your business real property to your SMSF; there is a statutory limit or cap on how much you can put into your super fund each year. So make sure the market value of the property does not breach the statutory limit or cap amount. For more details see the Tax Office publication *Key superannuation rates and thresholds*—'concessional contributions cap' and 'non-concessional contributions cap'.

Borrowing to buy a property

In September 2007 the federal government relaxed the rules prohibiting a SMSF from borrowing money to buy investment assets such as property. Provided certain conditions are satisfied, a SMSF can borrow using a limited recourse borrowing arrangement (or instalment warrant) to purchase investment assets such as commercial and residential property. Under this arrangement, the property is held in trust, and ownership cannot be transferred to your SMSF until the loan is fully discharged. Further, the loan must be structured on a limited recourse basis. This means if your super fund is unable to repay the loan, the lender will have no claim against your super fund's other assets to recover any outstanding amount. Any potential financial loss is effectively limited to the specific property. To do all this by the book it's best that you seek professional advice from a solicitor or registered tax agent. For more information see the Tax Office publications *Instalment warrants and super funds—questions and answers* and *Taxpayer Alert TA 2008/5—Certain borrowings by self managed superannuation funds*.

Useful references

- FIDO, the consumer website of the Australian Securities & Investments Commission <www.fido.gov.au>; go to 'About financial products', then click 'Unlisted investments'

Australian Taxation Office publications

- *Personal investors guide to capital gains tax (NAT 4152)*
- *Approved auditors and self-managed super funds*
- *TA 2008/5 — Certain borrowings by self-managed superannuation funds*

Australian Taxation Office interpretative decisions

- ID 2003/163: *Income tax: capital gains tax: main residence exemption — residence owned by company*
- ID 2003/467: *Income tax: capital gains tax: main residence exemption — residence owned by family trust*

Other taxation rulings

- TR 93/32: *Income tax: rental property — division of net income or loss between co-owners*
- IT 2316: *Distribution of partnership profits and losses*
- SMSFR 2009/1: *Self Managed Superannuation Funds: business real property for the purposes of the Superannuation Industry (Supervision) Act 1993*

Chapter 9

Keeping proper records and tax audits: Big Brother is watching you

Investors who own rental properties and property developers or property speculators who carry on a property business are required to maintain proper records of all their property transactions. Stiff penalties may apply if you fail to comply with your legal obligation to disclose the correct amount of taxable income you derive each year. Note: taxable income means assessable income less allowable deductions. So you'll need to keep account of both sides of the equation. In this chapter I emphasise the need to keep accurate records and point out the common mistakes the Tax Office looks out for if it audits your tax affairs.

Record keeping

Under Australian tax law you have a legal obligation to keep a record of your assessable income and expenses for five years after you lodge your annual tax return for individuals. According to the Income Tax Assessment Act your records must be kept in the English language and must be readily available for inspection in the event of a tax audit.

 Tax tip

Under Australian tax law the Tax Office has full and free access to all buildings, places, books, documents and other papers for the purposes of the Tax Act, and can make extracts from, or copies of, any such books, documents or papers. The Tax Office also has the authority to compel you to supply any relevant information for the purposes of the Tax Act. Stiff penalties apply if you fail to comply with this statutory requirement.

What you'll need to keep

You'll need to retain the following documents relating to your property transactions, and produce them if you're audited by the Tax Office.

Tax tip

Under the pay-as-you-go (PAYG) withholding tax system you may be required to prepare a business activity statement or instalment activity statement setting out the amount of rent you derive (and/or profits you make if you carry on a property business), and pay tax on an ongoing basis. Incidentally, any expenses you incur are ignored when preparing these statements. You'll need to keep accurate records to comply with this legal obligation. The Tax Office will notify you if you need to do this.

Contract of sale

The contract of sale will set out the date of purchase (or sale) and the purchase price (or sale price). Note: under the capital gains tax (CGT) provisions you're treated as having purchased (or sold) a property on the date of the signing of the contract of sale, rather than on the settlement date when legal ownership ordinarily changes hands. Other documents relating to the purchase and sale of a property include:

- *Contract note:* this is similar to the contract of sale and is ordinarily signed by the vendor and purchaser at the time of purchase or sale. This is normally prepared by a real estate agent

- *Settlement statement:* this document sets out the unexpired portion of any holding costs (such as council rates and land taxes) that a vendor receives from the purchaser at the time of purchase; incidentally, if the property is a rental property the amount you pay to the vendor is a tax-deductible expense; see appendix A, Settlement adjustments (sale of property)

- *Certificate of title:* a legal document setting out the description of the property and verifying that you are the legal owner; it's best that you keep this legal document in a safe place.

Incidental costs of purchase (sale)

If you are a property investor, keep a record of your incidental costs of purchase (and sale) such as stamp duty, agent commission, legal and accounting fees and costs of advertising or marketing to find a buyer. These costs are not tax deductible but can be added to the property's cost base. They can be taken into account when calculating whether you make a capital gain or capital loss on sale. On the other hand, if you're carrying on a property business, these costs are ordinarily tax-deductible expenses (see chapter 2).

Capital improvements

You should keep a record of any capital improvements you make to your properties and the dates you make them (for instance, you make improvements to the kitchen and bathroom). If you're a property investor, these costs are added to the cost base and are taken into account to calculate whether you have made a capital gain or capital loss for tax purposes (see chapter 4).

Loan documents

Keep all documents relating to financing the purchase of your rental property, and more particularly the interest repayments.

Rental lease agreements

You must keep a copy of the written rental lease agreement you entered into with your tenant (see chapter 1).

Rental statements

Keep a record of the rent you receive from your tenants. If you employ a real estate agent to collect the rent on your behalf, they will normally send you regular rental statements setting out the rent you receive. You will need this information if you're required to prepare quarterly business activity statements (BAS) or instalment activity statements.

Tax-deductible expenses

You'll need to keep receipts and invoices to verify and substantiate any rental expenses you incur in deriving your rental income (for instance, interest on borrowings and repairs). If you carry on a property business, you can claim certain expenses that are necessarily incurred in deriving your assessable income (trading profits), that are not ordinarily available to investors who own rental properties (see chapter 3).

Insurance policies

It's best that you take out insurance to cover for any potential loss or damage to your rental property. Insurance fees are tax-deductible expenses.

 Tax tip

It's best that you maintain a cheque account to record all the assessable income you derive each year from various sources (particularly your rental receipts), and all the ongoing tax-deductible expenses you incur (particularly your rental deductions). This will help you to quickly prepare your BAS or instalment activity statement each quarter and to calculate your taxable income at the end of the financial year.

Non-deductible holding costs

If you have bought a property since 20 August 1991 that you use primarily for private or domestic purposes (for instance, a holiday home or block of land), you should keep a record of all your non-deductible holding costs, such as interest on borrowings to buy the property, council rates and land taxes, insurance and repairs. Under the CGT provisions these costs can be added to the property's cost base, and can be taken into account if you make a capital gain on sale (see chapter 4).

Calculations

You must keep a record of how you calculate expenditure such as interest and borrowing costs and capital works deductions. You also have to keep a record of how you calculated any capital gains or capital losses you made on disposal of an investment property, holiday home or vacant block of land. Incidentally, you will find a capital gain or capital loss worksheet in the Tax Office publication *Guide to capital gains tax*, which you can use to correctly calculate a capital gain or capital loss. You will also need to show how you apportioned any expenditure that is partly investment-related and partly private. This could arise if you own a property that is partly used to derive assessable income; for instance, you own a shop that you use to derive assessable income and you reside at the back of the premises.

Schedules

You'll need to keep a depreciation schedule listing all your depreciable assets, the date of purchase, cost price, rate of depreciation and method used to record the amount you can claim each year and their adjusted values. You'll also need to keep a record of any valuations of depreciable items you've received from a qualified quantity surveyor.

 Tax tip

To help you maintain proper records you can set up a CGT asset register to help you keep track of all

Tax tip *(cont'd)*

the properties you own. If you want to do this; the information will need to be certified by a registered tax agent or a person approved by the Tax Office. For more details you can read the Tax Office publication *Guide to capital gains tax* (NAT 4151), and more particularly go to 'Keeping Records—Asset registers'. You can download a copy from the Tax Office website <www.ato.gov.au>.

Capital losses

If you are a property investor you'll need to keep a record of any capital losses you incur. This is because a capital loss can only be deducted from a capital gain. If you make no capital gains in the same financial year you incur a capital loss, the capital loss can be offset against future capital gains. Incidentally, a capital loss on the sale of a property can be deducted from a capital gain you may make on the sale of other CGT assets such as shares.

If you have unapplied capital losses from earlier years, you must offset any capital gains you make against the earlier years in the order you incur your capital losses. For instance, if you incurred a capital loss two years ago and a further capital loss one year ago, any capital gain you make on sale must first be applied against the capital loss you incurred two years ago and afterwards against the capital loss you incurred one year ago.

Tax audits

As was pointed out in chapter 1, Australia's tax system operates on a self-assessment basis. Under this system, when you lodge your annual income tax return, the Tax Office will ordinarily accept its contents as being true and correct. However, the Tax Office reserves the right to audit your tax affairs. It regularly conducts desk audits to check whether the information you disclosed in your tax return is in accordance with your personal records. The Tax Office also does regular data-matching checks where information disclosed in your tax return is matched with information obtained from various government agencies and external sources.

At a glance: what the Tax Office is checking

The Tax Office has advised that routine tax audits and data-matching programs (where data disclosed in tax returns are compared with external information) have revealed the following common mistakes relating to rental properties.

Rental income

Mistakes relating to rental income include:

- not declaring all the rental income you receive
- not declaring rental income on holiday homes.

Tax deductions

Mistakes relating to tax deductions include:

- overstating rental expenses

- claiming tax deductions for properties that are not genuinely available for rent (see chapter 3)

- overstating interest deductions by including amounts relating to borrowing costs (see chapter 7)

- claiming deductions for expenses relating to the private use of a property such as a holiday home

- incorrectly depreciating items (such as built-in wardrobes) that are deductible under the capital-works provisions (see chapter 3)

- incorrectly claiming borrowing costs in the financial year they're incurred rather than over the period of the loan, or five years (see chapter 7)

- incorrectly apportioning interest deductions for loans that are partly investment-related and partly private

- incorrectly claiming travel expenses to inspect the property when the trip is also partly for private purposes

- incorrectly claiming capital-works deductions that exceed the construction expenditure (see chapter 3)

- incorrectly claiming the cost of the land as a capital-works deduction item (see chapter 3)

- claiming a tax deduction for conveyancing costs

- claiming initial repairs as repairs and maintenance costs, rather than including the costs as part of the property's cost base (see chapter 3)

- not claiming partial deductions when a property is only rented out for part of the year — this calculation is ordinarily done on a time basis.

Capital gains tax

Mistakes relating to capital gains tax include:

- not declaring capital gains on the sale of rental properties, holiday homes and vacant land (see chapter 4)

- incorrectly calculating a capital gain or capital loss; using the settlement date for the disposal of a property rather than the date of the signing of the contract of sale (see chapter 4)

- incorrectly claiming a main-residence exemption when you've never lived in the property (see chapter 5).

Record keeping

Mistakes relating to record keeping include:

- keeping poor records (for instance, not keeping proper receipts for claims for repairs, interest and insurance expenses).

If any errors are detected (for instance, you understate your rental income and/or overstate your rental expenses), the Tax Office will amend your tax return and penalties may apply.

 Tax trap

Keep in mind the Tax Office performs ongoing audit checks by comparing the information you have disclosed with external information obtained from various government agencies and external sources. So chances are the system will eventually weed you out if you fail to disclose any rental income you receive or any capital gains you make on the sale of an investment property, holiday home or vacant block of land. For more details see the Tax Office publication *Compliance program 2009–10 (NAT 7769)*.

Under Australian tax law the Tax Office has the power to amend an assessment that it considers to be incorrect. Generally, there is a time limit of between two and four years from the date the tax became due and payable. You also have the right to seek an amendment (for instance, you forgot to claim some rental expenses).

Further, you can lodge an objection if you're dissatisfied with a Tax Office decision or your notice of assessment. If you do this and your objection is subsequently disallowed, you have a further right to appeal to the Administrative Appeals Tribunal — Small Taxation Claims Tribunal or Tax Appeals Division. And if you're still dissatisfied you can go all the way to the High Court of Australia if the dispute relates to a question of law.

Useful references

Australian Taxation Office publications

- *Keeping your tax records*
- *Record keeping for CGT*
- *Tax audits — what are they?*

Other taxation rulings

- TR 2002/10: *Income tax: capital gains tax: asset register*
- TR 96/7: *Income tax record keeping general principles* (section 262A)

Glossary

active asset An asset such as your business premises or factory that you use to derive assessable income. If you operate a small business and make a capital gain on the sale of an active asset, the capital gain can be reduced to nil.

allowable deduction An expense you can deduct from your assessable income.

approved auditor A qualified accountant who's authorised to audit self managed superannuation funds.

assessable distribution A distribution you receive from a property trust that's liable to income tax.

assessable income   Income you derive that is liable to income tax. Assessable income consists of ordinary income and statutory income (per Australian taxation legislation).

Australian business number (ABN)   The number you quote whenever you conduct a business transaction. If you derive rental income you don't need to quote this number to your tenant.

Australian Securities Exchange (ASX)   Australia's major market securities exchange responsible for regulating and controlling the buying and selling of Australian-listed securities such as shares.

Australian Taxation Office (ATO)   The federal government authority that's responsible for administering the Income Tax Assessment Act.

beneficiary   A person who is entitled to receive a distribution from a trust.

borrowing costs   Costs you incur when you borrow money to buy a property. If you buy an income-producing property, borrowing costs that exceed $100 must be spread over the period of the loan or over five years if the period of the loan is more than five years.

bridging loan   A short-term loan that you take out to cover your position while another financial transaction you have entered into is in the course of being completed.

business activity statement (BAS)   A statement under the pay-as-you-go system that you prepare at the end of each reporting period (usually quarterly) disclosing certain income (for instance rent) that is liable to tax.

business real property A business premises such as a shop, office or factory that you use to derive your assessable income.

capital Funds used to conduct business operations, or money invested in assets such as a rental property.

capital gain A gain you make when you sell CGT assets such as property for a price that's greater than its cost base. Under Australian tax law a capital gain is liable to capital gains tax. The way you calculate a capital gain changed on 21 September 1999.

capital gains tax (CGT) A tax on capital gains you make on disposal of CGT assets such as property that you acquire on or after 20 September 1985.

capital growth An increase in the value of your investment.

capital loss The loss you incur when you sell CGT assets, such as property, for a price that's below its reduced cost base. Under Australian tax law a capital loss can only be offset against a capital gain.

capital proceeds The sale price of a CGT asset such as property.

capital-works deduction A specific tax deduction you can claim for the construction costs of an income-producing property, or any improvements or extensions you make to an income-producing property.

carrying on a property business   Carrying on business as a property developer/speculator (such as buying, building and renovating properties) with the predominant purpose of making a profit. This could also be the case if you manage and maintain a large number of rental properties.

certificate of title   A legal document setting out the description of your property and verifying that you are the legal owner of that property.

CGT asset   An asset such as property that you've acquired since 20 September 1985 that's liable to tax under the capital gains tax provisions.

CGT asset register   A register you keep to record all CGT assets you own, such as your property portfolio.

CGT-concession distributions   Distributions that are not assessable to unit holders. Under the CGT provisions they are not deducted from the unit's cost base or reduced cost base.

CGT event   Normally arises when there's a change in ownership of a CGT-asset such as property (for instance when you sell a property or give it to someone).

commission   A fee you pay to a real estate agent for selling your property or to collect the rent on your behalf.

company   A legal entity that can carry on a business and own property in its own name. A company raises capital to fund its business operations through the issue of shares. A company pays a 30 per cent rate of tax on every taxable dollar it derives.

complying superannuation fund   A fund that has agreed to be regulated under the Superannuation Industry (Supervision) Act. Complying super funds are taxed at the rate of 15 per cent and can pay pensions to their members.

condition of release   A condition you must satisfy before you can access your benefits in a superannuation fund. The most common condition is when you retire.

consumer price index (CPI)   An index that Australia uses to calculate its rate of inflation.

contract note   A legal document that is ordinarily signed by the vendor and purchaser at the time of a property sale.

contract of sale   A legal document that's normally prepared by a solicitor setting out the sale price and the terms and conditions of the sale of a property.

cost base   The price you pay for CGT assets such as property, under the capital gains tax provisions. It also includes your acquisition and disposal costs (for instance, stamp duty and agent's commission).

council rates   A tax levied on property owners by local government authorities to help fund local government services (such as rubbish collection).

crystallise   Dispose of property in order to create or realise a capital gain or capital loss for taxation purposes.

decline in value   A Tax Office term for depreciation.

deposit   A down payment you make at the time you purchase a property. The payment is normally 10 per cent of the purchase price.

depreciation   The process of writing off the value of assets you use to derive your assessable income. Under tax law this is referred to as a decline in value.

derived income   Income you receive or earn that's liable to tax.

desk audit   A tax audit where the Tax Office asks you to visit them and produce documentary evidence to verify the accuracy of your individual tax return.

diminishing value method (DVM)   An accounting method used to work out the rate of depreciation you can claim each year. Under this method you can claim a larger amount in earlier years and a lesser amount in later years.

discount capital gain   A capital gain on disposal of a CGT asset such as property that was owned for at least 12 months. Only half the capital gain you make on disposal is liable to tax. The other half is exempt.

discretionary trust   A trust where the trustee has discretion as to how the trust net income should be distributed to the beneficiaries.

e-tax   A free electronic lodgement service provided by the Tax Office to allow you to lodge your tax return online.

family discretionary trust   A trust whose membership is ordinarily made up of family beneficiaries. The trustee has discretion to distribute trust net income to certain family beneficiaries.

financial planner   A licensed professional who can give you financial advice and prepare an investment plan.

financial year   Australia's financial year, commencing 1 July and ending 30 June.

first home owner grant   A federal government initiative to help first home buyers buy or build their first home. Under this scheme, first home owners normally receive a one-off payment of $7000 to purchase or build a property they intend to use as their main residence.

first home saver accounts   A federal government initiative to help first home buyers to save for a deposit to buy or build their first home.

fixed-rate loan   A loan where the rate of interest is fixed for a certain period of time.

foreign income tax offset   Foreign tax paid on income derived from overseas sources that can be offset against Australian tax payable on income derived from worldwide sources.

goods and services tax (GST)   A 10 per cent tax on goods and services on your purchases and sales. No GST is payable on rent you receive from residential property used predominantly for residential accommodation.

GST credit   A refund of the 10 per cent goods and services tax you incur on your costs or inputs.

holiday home   A property that you keep primarily for your personal use and enjoyment.

home loan   A loan to purchase your main residence. It will have specific features tailored to suit your particular circumstances.

incidental costs   Costs associated with buying and selling a property. These can include costs such as stamp duty, agent commissions, legal and accounting fees and costs of advertising or marketing to find a buyer. These costs can be added to the cost base.

income tax   A federal tax that you pay on taxable income you derive, such as rent.

Income Tax Assessment Act   A collection of various tax acts that give the federal government the authority to levy a tax on taxable income.

income tax return   A form you lodge with the Australian Taxation Office each year disclosing your taxable income.

incurred   The point in time when you can legally claim a tax deduction. This normally arises when you're definitely committed and have a legal obligation to make a payment for certain goods and services you receive.

indexed cost base   The purchase price of a CGT asset you acquired prior to 30 September 1999, plus certain costs you incur that have been adjusted for inflation.

initial repairs   Repairs you make to a newly acquired property. These repairs are not tax-deductible expenses.

input tax credit   A refund of the 10 per cent goods and services tax that you incur on your acquisitions.

instalment activity statement   A statement under the pay-as-you-go system that you prepare at the end of each reporting period disclosing certain income that is liable to tax.

interest-only loan   A loan where you're only required to repay interest over a certain period of time. The principal is repaid at a later date or when the loan matures.

interpretative decision   An Australian Taxation Office ruling relating to a specific tax issue.

investment strategy   A document that sets out how you intend to invest your benefits in a self managed super-annuation fund. It must be in writing and must consider investment risks, the likely return on your investments, and whether you've got sufficient cash on hand to discharge liabilities when they fall due.

joint ownership   Owning investments jointly (for instance, as husband and wife).

land tax   A state government tax paid on property holdings such as a rental property or holiday home.

line of credit loan   A loan where you can access finance up to an approved predetermined limit.

low-doc loans   A loan where no documentary evidence is required to verify your capacity to make payments. They are normally offered to high-risk investors at a high rate of interest.

low-income tax offset   A general tax offset you can claim if your taxable income is below a taxable income threshold (currently $30 000). The tax offset is reduced by four cents for every dollar you earn above this threshold.

low value pool   A method of depreciation where you can pool (accumulate) all depreciable items that cost less than $1000.

main residence   The place where you normally reside. It can also include up to two hectares of land that surround your home. Your main residence is normally exempt from tax under the capital gains tax provisions.

managed fund   Mutual or pooled investment funds managed by Australia's leading financial institutions (such as banks and insurance companies) that give investors the opportunity to invest in a wide range of domestic and foreign investment portfolios.

marginal rate of tax   The rate of tax payable on the last taxable-income dollar you earn. The rate can vary from between 0 per cent to 45 per cent (see Tax Office website for latest published rates).

market value   The price a buyer is willing but not anxious to pay to a vendor who in turn is willing but not anxious to sell if the property was up for sale on the open market.

Medicare levy   A medical levy based on a percentage of your taxable income (currently 1.5 per cent).

negative gearing A term associated with borrowing money to buy wealth-creation assets such as property. You are negative gearing when your expenses (particularly interest payments) exceed the income you derive.

net income The amount of income that's left over when you deduct your allowable deductions from your assessable income.

net loss A loss that arises when your allowable deductions exceed your assessable income.

nil consideration A term to indicate you received nothing in return for giving or transferring a CGT asset such as property to someone (for instance, to your child).

non-deductible holding costs Non-deductible expenditure such as interest that can be included in the cost base of non-income-producing property acquired on or after 20 August 1991.

non-discount capital gain A capital gain on disposal of a CGT asset that you have owned for less than 12 months. The entire capital gain is liable to tax.

non-resident of Australia A person who does not normally reside in Australia and has no intention of living here. Non-residents are liable to pay tax only on income sourced in Australia.

notice of assessment The statement you receive from the Tax Office after you lodge your tax return summarising the details in your tax return.

notional capital gain   A temporary or unofficial gain that exists until the actual amount of the capital gain that's liable to tax has been determined.

objection   A formal challenge against a Tax Office assessment or decision.

occupancy expenses   Expenses that relate to occupying a property such as rent, interest on a mortgage, council rates, insurance and repairs.

partnership   Under Australian tax law persons in receipt of income jointly are considered to be in partnership.

pay-as–you-go (PAYG) withholding tax   Employers have a statutory obligation to withhold a certain amount of tax from an employee's pay and remit the amount to the Tax Office.

personal loan   Normally an unsecured loan that you can take out for a specific purpose (for instance, to buy property).

positive gearing   A term associated with borrowing money to buy wealth-creation assets such as property. You are positive gearing when your investment income (cash inflows) exceeds your investment expenses (cash outflows).

presently entitled   The right of a beneficiary of a trust to demand an immediate distribution of the trust's net income.

preservation age   The age you must reach before you can access your superannuation fund benefits. Depending on when you're born this can vary from 55 to 60 years of age.

preserved benefits   Superannuation fund benefits that you can access when you reach your preservation age and retire.

prime cost method (PCM)   An accounting method where you can work out a fixed amount of depreciation that you can claim each year.

principal plus interest loan   A loan where you'll pay back both interest and principal at regular intervals (for instance, fortnightly or monthly).

private ruling   Written advice you can get from the Tax Office outlining how they would interpret the tax laws relating to a specific issue you raise.

product disclosure statement   A legal document that must be prepared when raising finance. It will set out relevant information about the investment products, the benefits and risks, and fees you'll be charged.

property   Real estate such as residential premises and commercial premises.

property investor   Someone whose primary reason for buying an investment property is to derive rent, and under the CGT provisions, your property holdings are treated as CGT assets.

property trust   A managed fund that invests pre-dominantly in major residential and commercial property developments located throughout Australia.

real estate   Property such as your main residence, blocks of land, shops, business premises, shopping centres and factories.

real estate agents   Professionals who are authorised to buy and sell real estate and collect the rent on your behalf. They charge a commission for their services.

reduced cost base   Similar to the cost base of a CGT asset minus certain expenditure that had been allowed as a tax deduction. It's used to calculate a capital loss.

rent   Money you receive from a tenant for the use of your property. Under Australian tax law this is referred to as income from property.

rental property   An investment property that you lease to receive rent from a tenant.

resident of Australia   A person who normally resides in Australia (it can also include a company or trust). Residents are taxed on their worldwide income.

Residential Tendencies Act   An act that gives state and territory governments the authority to regulate the rights and obligations of landlords and tenants.

S&P/ASX 200 index   A Standard and Poor's index that comprises the top 200 companies/property trusts that are listed on the Australian Securities Exchange (ASX).

self-assessment   The Australian tax system works on a self-assessment basis. This means the onus is on you to declare to the Tax Office the correct amount of income you derive each year and claim the correct amount of tax deductions and tax offsets.

self managed superannuation fund (SMSF)   A superannuation fund that you set up and manage yourself.

settlement statement   A document, normally prepared by a solicitor, setting out the unexpired portion of any holding costs (such as council rates and land taxes) that the vendor receives from the purchaser at the time of purchase.

stamp duty   a state or territory government tax that applies to certain property transactions, such as when you buy a property.

superannuation fund   A fund set up to finance retirement strategies. Benefits cannot normally be accessed until you reach your preservation age and retire from the workforce. A superannuation fund can pay you a pension.

tax agent   A person who is authorised to give you advice on managing your tax affairs and can lodge a tax return on your behalf. The fee they charge for their services is a tax-deductible expense.

tax-deferred distribution   A distribution that is not assessable to unit holders. Under the CGT provisions it is deducted from the unit's cost base or reduced cost base.

tax file number (TFN)   A number you get from the Australian Taxation Office. You may need to quote this number to companies that pay unfranked dividends.

tax-free distribution   A distribution that is not assessable to unit holders. Under the CGT provisions it is deducted from the unit's reduced cost base when calculating a capital loss.

tax-exempted distribution   A distribution that is not assessable to unit holders. Under the CGT provisions it is not deducted from the cost base or reduced cost base.

tax offset   A tax credit or rebate that you can use to reduce the amount of tax payable on taxable income you derive.

tax refund   Money you get back from the Tax Office if your total tax credits (tax previously paid plus tax offsets) exceed the amount of tax you are liable to pay.

tax ruling   A public ruling issued by the Tax Office to explain and clarify how the Tax Office interprets tax legislation in respect of a specific issue.

taxable Australian property   Assets (such as real estate) owned by non-residents of Australia that are located in Australia and liable to capital gains tax when they are disposed of.

taxable income   The amount of income that's liable to tax. Taxable income equals assessable income less allowable deductions.

tenants in common   A term associated with owning real estate jointly (for instance, as business partners). In the event of death, legal title to the property can be transferred to the deceased's beneficiaries.

termination value   The sale price of a depreciable item.

trust   A legal obligation binding a person (the trustee) who has control over investment assets (for instance, a rental property) for the benefit of beneficiaries.

trustee   A person responsible for administering and managing the trust property over which he or she has control for the benefit of the beneficiaries.

under a legal disability   Indicates that a beneficiary of a trust is not in a legal position to deal with a trust distribution, such as a minor, bankrupt or mentally incompetent person.

unit holders   Investors who own units in a managed fund.

variable-rate loan   A loan where interest rates will vary in line with the prevailing market.

vendor finance loans   A loan where the vendor (for instance, a property developer) provides the necessary finance to the purchaser to buy a property.

yield   The return you receive on your investment expressed as a percentage.

Appendix A

Key tax cases relating to property and taxation

The following famous tax cases are often quoted and relied upon as authorities when dealing with common property and taxation issues. You can find these cases on the Tax Office website <www.ato.gov.au>.

Active asset (deriving rent)
Carson & anor v FC of T 2008 ATC 10-006
Tingari Village North Pty Ltd v FC of T 2010
   ATC 10-131

Apportionment of rental deductions
Fletcher & ors v FC of T 91 ATC 4950

FC of T v Kowal 84 ATC 4001
Madigan v FC of T 96 ATC 4640
Ure v FC of T 81 ATC 4100

Borrowing funds (purpose or use test)
FC of T v Munro (1926) 38 CLR 153

Business activity (or mere realisation of capital asset)
Casimaty v FC of T 97 ATC 5135
FC of T v Williams 72 ATC 4188
Scottish Australian Mining Co Ltd v FC of T (1950)
    81 CLR 188
Statham v FC of T 89 ATC 4070
Stevenson v FC of T 91 ATC 4476
Whitfords Beach Pty Ltd v FC of T 82 ATC 4031

Co-owned rental property
Cripps v FC of T 1999 ATC 2428
FC of T v McDonald 87 ATC 4541

Demolishing buildings
Mount Isa Mines Ltd v FC of T 92 ATC 4755

Depreciation deductions
FC of T v Mount Isa Mines Ltd 91 ATC 4154
*Imperial Chemical Industries of Australia and
    New Zealand v FC of T* 70 ATC 4024
Wangaratta Woollen Mills v FC of T 69 ATC 4095
Yarmouth v France (1887) 19 QBD 647

Derivation of income
(sale of property — settlement date)
Benwerrin Developments Pty Ltd v FC of T 81 ATC 4524
Gasparin v FC of T 94 ATC 4280

Forfeiture of deposit (sale of property)
Brooks v FC of T 2000 ATC 4362
FC of T v Guy 96 ATC 4520
FC of T v Reliance Carpet Co Pty Ltd 2008 ATC 20-028

Goods & services tax (input tax credit)
Sunchen Pty Ltd v FC of T 2008 ATC 10-070
Touram Pty Ltd v FC of T 2010 ATC 20-161

Goods & services tax (property)
Brady King Pty Ltd v FC of T 2008 ATC 20-008
Marana Holdings Pty v FC of T 2004 ATC 5068
South Steyne Hotel Pty Ltd v FC of T 2009   ATC 20-090
Vidler v FC of T 2010 ATC 20-186

Home office deductions
FC of T v Faichney 72 ATC 4245
FC of T v Forsyth 81 ATC 4157
Handley v FC of T 81 ATC 4165
Swinford v FC of T 84 ATC 4803

Intention to lease (claiming a tax deduction)
Ormiston v FC of T 2005 ATC 2340

Interest deductions (after cessation of income)
FC of T v Brown 99 ATC 4600

FC of T v Jones 2002 ATC 4135
Placer Pacific Management Pty Ltd v FC of T 95 ATC 4459

Interest deductions (general principles)
FC of T v Carberry 88 ATC 5005
FC of T v Ilbery 81 ATC 4661
FC of T v Roberts and Smith 92 ATC 4380
Temelli v FC of T 97 ATC 4716

Interest deductions (prior to derivation of income)
Anovoy Pty Ltd v FC of T 2001 ATC 4197
Steele v FC of T 99 ATC 4242
Travelodge Papua New Guinea Ltd v Chief Collector of Taxes 85 ATC 4432

Isolated transactions (profit motive)
FC of T v Myer Emporium Ltd 87 ATC 4363
Moana Sand v FC of T 88 ATC 4897

Land & trading stock
Barina Corporation Ltd v FC of T 85 ATC 4847
FC of T v Kurts Development Ltd 98 ATC 4877
FC of T v St Hubert's Island Pty Ltd 78 ATC 4104

Lease incentives
FC of T v Cooling 90 ATC 4472
FC of T v Montgomery 99 ATC 4749
Lees & Leech Pty Ltd v FC of T 97 ATC 4407
Selleck v FC of T 97 ATC 4856

Lease surrender (receipts & payments)

Kennedy Holdings and Property Management Pty Ltd v FC of T 92 ATC 4918

Rotherwood v FC of T 96 ATC 4203

Main-residence exemption

Caller & anor v FC of T 2009   ATC 10-116

Chapman v FC of T 2008 ATC 10-029

Couch v FC of T 2009 ATC 10-072

Erdelyi v FC of T 2007 ATC 2214

Maintenance of rental property (not carrying on a business)

Cripps v FC of T 1999 ATC 2428

Market value (meaning)

Abrahams v FC of T (1944) 70 CLR 23

Spencer v Commonwealth (1907) 5 CLR 418

Non-commercial rent (leasing property at below market rate)

FC of T v Groser 82 ATC 4478

Place of residence (meaning)

Koitaki Para Rubber Estates Ltd v FC of T (1941) 64 CLR 241

Profit-making purpose

Crow v FC of T 88 ATC 4620

Kratzmann v FC of T 70 ATC 4043

Property (genuinely available for rent)
Bonaccordo v FC of T 2009 ATC 10-092
Inglis v FC of T 87 ATC 3037

Repairs
FC of T v Western Suburbs Cinemas Ltd (1952)
    86 CLR 102
Law Shipping Co Ltd v IRC (1924) 12 TC 621
Lindsay v FC of T (1961) 106 CLR 377
Lucott v Wakely & Wheeler (1911) KB 905
W Thomas & Co Pty Ltd v FC of T (1965)
    115 CLR 58

Security costs (security locks & external lighting installed in family home)
Frankcom v FC of T 82 ATC 4599

Settlement adjustments (sale of property)
FC of T v Morgan (1961) 106 CLR 517
Goldsbrough Mort & Co Ltd v FC of T 76 ATC 4343

Split loan facilities
Hart v FC of T 2004 ATC 4599

Travel costs (inspect rental properties)
FC of T v Green (1950) CLR 313

Trusts (& negative gearing)
FC of T v Janmor Nominees Pty Ltd 87 ATC 4813
Tabone v FC of T 2006 ATC 2211

Index